Introduction to Quantitative Economics

Introduction to Quantitative Economics

Jesse M. Shapiro

The MIT Press
Cambridge, Massachusetts
London, England

The MIT Press
Massachusetts Institute of Technology
77 Massachusetts Avenue
Cambridge, MA 02139
mitpress.mit.edu

The MIT Press would like to thank the anonymous peer reviewers who provided comments on drafts of this book. The generous work of academic experts is essential for establishing the authority and quality of our publications. We acknowledge with gratitude the contributions of these otherwise uncredited readers.

This book was set in Times New Roman by Westchester Publishing Services. Printed and bound in the United States of America.

Library of Congress Cataloging-in-Publication Data is available.

ISBN: 978-0-262-05105-7

10 9 8 7 6 5 4 3 2

EU product safety and compliance information contact is: mitp-eu-gpsr@mit.edu

Contents

Preface

This course aims to introduce graduate students to quantitative economics, by which I mean the use of economic models to interpret data. The course assumes knowledge of economic and econometric theory at the level of an introductory graduate sequence.

The course proceeds through a series of economic settings. Each setting motivates a canonical economic model. Students are asked to reflect on a set of questions, to read proposed answers, and then to perform some exercises. Exercises are a combination of theoretical exercises designed to extend concepts and quantitative exercises designed to apply them.

At the end of the course, students are prepared to begin using economic theory to interpret data. They are also prepared to continue the study of quantitative economics within particular subfields, where they may encounter more elaborate or specialized economic models, and more complex data structures.

The course relies heavily on student work. Students who do not pause to consider (and, ideally, write answers to) the reflection questions, or who do not work through the exercises, are likely to get much less out of the course than students who make those investments.

The methodological perspective of the course builds on Marschak (1950). I learned many of the specific models in the book from my teachers, some of whom have written textbooks (see, e.g., Becker 2007; Jaffe et al. 2019). Former teaching assistants and students have also contributed to the development of the course.

Introduction

Quantitative economics is concerned with the use of economic models to interpret data. Its role is illustrated in the following stylized workflow.

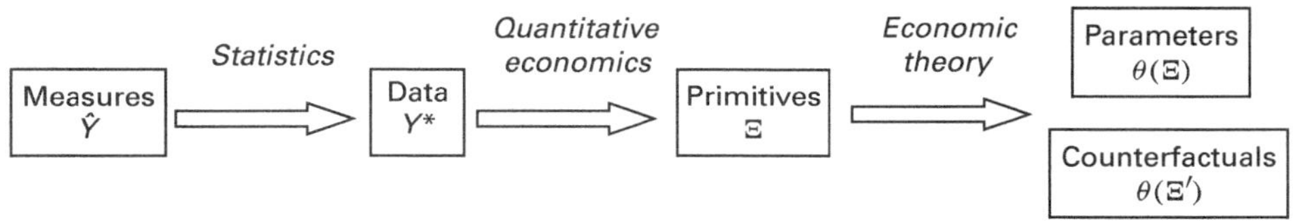

Some measures $\hat{Y}$ are obtained for some economic data Y^*. For example, we may measure incomes $\hat{Y}$ for a sample of individuals in a population with income distribution Y^*. An important task of statistics is to help make inferences about the economic data Y^* from the measures $\hat{Y}$, for example by using a model of the sampling process to learn about the population distribution of income from the sample distribution of income.

Under some economic model, the data Y^* can be informative about some economic primitives Ξ. For example, knowledge of the population distribution of income may inform some primitives that govern the income process. An important task of quantitative economics is to make inferences about the primitives Ξ from the data Y^*. Economic theory may then be used to derive a parameter of interest $\theta(\Xi)$, such as the efficiency of the economy, or a counterfactual instance $\theta\left(\Xi'\right)$ of the parameter under alternative primitives, such as an income tax.

This course will be especially concerned with when and how we can learn primitives Ξ, parameters $\theta(\Xi)$, and counterfactuals $\theta\left(\Xi'\right)$ of interest from economic data Y^*. The course will touch occasionally on issues of measurement, and on themes adjacent to statistics, but these will not be front and center.

1

Monopoly

A firm sells a distinctive good at some price $P^* > 0$ to a population of customers. The firm sells a quantity $Q^* = Q(P^*) > 0$ determined by the strictly decreasing and differentiable demand function $Q : \mathbb{R}_{\geq 0} \to \mathbb{R}_{\geq 0}$. For simplicity's sake, we suppose that the firm has a constant marginal cost $C > 0$ of production. An example of a good sold in this way might be a subscription from the local cable company, or an on-patent drug.

Our data consist of $\{P^*, Q^*\}$, that is, the price of the good and the quantity sold. We, the economist, posit that the firm is a monopolist that maximizes static profits given by $\pi(P) = Q(P)(P - C)$, possibly up to a fixed cost that does not depend on the price or quantity sold.

Definition 1.1. The *static monopoly model* holds that

$$P^* \in \arg\max_{P \in \mathbb{R}_{\geq 0}} \pi(P)$$

$$\pi(P) = Q(P)(P - C)$$

$$Q^* = Q(P^*).$$

It is a property of the static monopoly model that $P^* > C$.[1]

1.1 Refuting the Model

If the model is inconsistent with the data then we may want to rethink the model. Therefore a first question we should ask is whether or when the model can be refuted.

> **Question 1.1.** *From data $\{P^*, Q^*\}$, can we ever refute the static monopoly model?*
>
> *Pause to reflect. Write down your answer before continuing.*

First we should probably say what it means for data to refute a model.

Definition 1.2. Consider a *model* that specifies a set $\mathcal{Y}(\Xi)$ of admissible values of some observed data Y given primitives Ξ. A given realization Y^* of the data *refutes* the model if there are no primitives Ξ such that $Y^* \in \mathcal{Y}(\Xi)$.

In the setting we are considering here, the data are $Y^* = \{P^*, Q^*\}$, the primitives are $\Xi = \{Q(\cdot), C\}$, and the model is the static monopoly model that specifies a set of feasible pairs $\{P, Q\}$ for any primitives Ξ.

From data on market price and quantity alone, we cannot refute the static monopoly model. Exercise 1.1 verifies this formally. Intuitively, since we have put very few restrictions on the model, it is always possible to find some primitives to justify any price-quantity pair.

It may help to enrich what we can measure. What if we we could observe the demand function $Q(\cdot)$?

Question 1.2. *From data $\{P^*, Q(\cdot)\}$, can we ever refute the static monopoly model?*

Pause to reflect. Write down your answer before continuing.

It may seem strange to think of a function $Q(\cdot)$ as part of our data, and indeed it is a bit strange, since we will rarely if ever measure such a rich object directly in the real world. For now we can view it as a kind of bookend for what we could hope to learn about the demand function. If we can't refute the model even with full knowledge of $Q(\cdot)$, then we can't refute it with the incomplete information about $Q(\cdot)$ that we can more realistically expect. If, on the other hand, full knowledge of $Q(\cdot)$ does allow us to refute the model, then understanding how may point the way toward relaxing the requirements for the data.

And, indeed, the model can be refuted in this case. To see how, recall that a necessary condition for an optimal price $P^* > 0$ is that

$$\pi'(P^*) = 0,$$

which can be written as

$$\frac{P^* - C}{P^*} = -\frac{Q^*}{P^* Q'(P^*)} = \frac{1}{-\varepsilon(P^*)}, \tag{1.1}$$

where $Q^* = Q(P^*)$ and $\varepsilon(P^*) < 0$ is the price elasticity of demand evaluated at price P^*. This is the famous Lerner Rule for optimal monopoly pricing.

Because $P^* > C > 0$ it is immediate that $\varepsilon(P^*) < -1$, or that the monopolist prices on the elastic part of the demand curve. Therefore if $Q(\cdot)$ is such that $-1 \leq \varepsilon(P^*) < 0$, the static monopoly model is refuted. It follows that, to have the prospect of refuting the model, it is not necessary to measure the entire demand function $Q(\cdot)$. Measuring its derivative local to the observed price P^* is sufficient.

Fact 1.1. From data $\{P^*, Q^*, Q'(P^*)\}$ it is possible to refute the static monopoly model, in particular if $-Q'(P^*) \leq \frac{Q^*}{P^*}$.

Fact 1.1 is useful in evaluating claims of monopolization. For example, typical estimates indicate that world oil demand is inelastic even in the long run (Smith, 2009). This refutes the hypothesis that the world oil market is monopolized, for example by OPEC. Fact 1.1 holds under more general forms of the monopolist's cost function. Exercise 1.2 shows this.

Fact 1.1 also illustrates a more general principle of quantitative economics.

> **Principle 1.** *Economic models impose restrictions on economic data, and these restrictions are useful in distinguishing among different models.*

1.2 Learning from the Model

Monopoly can lead to economic inefficiency because pricing a good above its marginal cost precludes some transactions that would benefit both the buyer and the seller. Beginning at the monopoly quantity Q^*, the gain in surplus from an incremental (infinitesimal) increase in the quantity is given by

$$\lambda = P^* - C, \tag{1.2}$$

which is also the monopolist's per-unit profit. Intuitively, P^* represents the value to the buyer of an incremental sale and C represents its cost to the seller.[2]

Knowing the value of λ may be useful, for example to evaluate the potential benefit from quantity regulation or competition policy. It is obvious that knowledge of P^* and C is sufficient to learn λ. In some markets it may be a tall order to ask the economist to measure the monopolist's marginal cost directly. Can we do without it?

Question 1.3. *From data $\{P^*, Q^*\}$, can we identify λ under the static monopoly model?*

Pause to reflect. Write down your answer before continuing.

First we should probably say what it means to identify an economic parameter.

Definition 1.3. Consider a model that, given primitives Ξ, specifies a set $\mathcal{Y}(\Xi)$ of admissible values of some observed data, and a value $\theta(\Xi)$ of some parameter. The parameter θ is *identified* if $Y^* \in \mathcal{Y}(\Xi), \mathcal{Y}(\Xi') \implies \theta(\Xi) = \theta(\Xi')$. That is, the parameter is identified if primitives that can yield identical data always imply identical values of the parameter.

In the setting we are considering here, the data are $Y^* = \{P^*, Q^*\}$, the primitives are $\Xi = \{Q(\cdot), C\}$, the parameter is the incremental gain in surplus λ, and the model is the static monopoly model.

From data on market price and quantity alone, we cannot identify the incremental gain in surplus λ. (Exercise 1.3 proves a stronger form of this statement.) What if we could measure something more about the demand function?

Question 1.4. *From data* $\{P^*, Q^*, Q'(P^*)\}$, *can we identify* λ *under the static monopoly model?*

Pause to reflect. Write down your answer before continuing.

The reasoning behind fact 1.1 is helpful here. From data $\{P^*, Q^*, Q'(P^*)\}$, we know the elasticity $\varepsilon(P^*)$ of demand at the equilibrium price P^*. From equation (1.1), we therefore know the Lerner index $(P^* - C)/P^*$, and hence we know the cost C from the price P^*. It follows that the answer to question 1.4 is yes.

Fact 1.2. Under the static monopoly model, the cost C, and therefore the incremental gain in surplus λ, is identified from data $\{P^*, Q^*, Q'(P^*)\}$.

Fact 1.2 is useful because it allows the economist to learn the incremental surplus λ without direct information on the monopolist's costs. For example, if we know the demand $Q(\cdot)$ for a drug sold by a monopoly patent-holder, we can assess the incremental surplus from a regulated increase in quantity sold without direct information on the costs of manufacturing and distribution. Exercise 1.4 shows that a statement similar to fact 1.2 holds for the incremental gain in surplus from a reduction in price.

Fact 1.2 also illustrates a more general principle of quantitative economics.

Principle 2. *Economic models tie together different economic objects, and these ties can make it easier to learn what we want to know.*

Principle 2 is important in part because often what we seek to know is not directly observable.

Definition 1.4. Consider a model that, given primitives Ξ, specifies a value $\theta(\Xi)$ of some economic object. Consider an alternative model that, given primitives $\tilde{\Xi}$, specifies a value $\tilde{\theta}\left(\tilde{\Xi}\right)$ of the same object. Then the *counterfactual* change in θ, given by $\tilde{\theta}\left(\tilde{\Xi}\right) - \theta(\Xi)$, is the change in the value of θ brought about by changing the primitives from Ξ to $\tilde{\Xi}$ and the model from $\theta(\cdot)$ to $\tilde{\theta}(\cdot)$.

For example, equation (1.2) gives the counterfactual change in total surplus if we hold the primitives $\Xi = \{Q(\cdot), C\}$ constant but modify the model to set the quantity incrementally above the one set by the static monopolist.

Exercises

Exercise 1.1. There exists no realization $\{P^*, Q^*\} \in \mathbb{R}^2_{\geq 0}$ that refutes the static monopoly model. Prove this.

Definition 1.5. The **generalized static monopoly model** holds that

$$P^* \in \arg\max_{P \in \mathbb{R}_{\geq 0}} \pi(P)$$

$$\pi(P) = Q(P)P - C(Q(P))$$

$$Q^* = Q(P^*)$$

for $C : \mathbb{R}_{\geq 0} \to \mathbb{R}_{\geq 0}$, a differentiable and strictly increasing total cost function.

Exercise 1.2. Fact 1.1 holds under the generalized static monopoly model. Prove this.

Exercise 1.3. Under the static monopoly model, the incremental gain in surplus λ is not identified from data $\{P^*, Q^*\}$. In particular, for any such data with $P^*, Q^* > 0$, any incremental gain in surplus $0 < \lambda < P^*$ is consistent with the static monopoly model. Prove this.

Exercise 1.4. Under the static monopoly model, an analogue of fact 1.2 holds for the incremental gain in surplus from a reduction in the price P^*. Prove this.

Exercise 1.5. Table 1.1 shows data on the global price and quantity of vitamin C for two years in the 1990s. An economist posits the model $Q_t = Q(P_t)$ for $Q(\cdot)$ a strictly decreasing and differentiable demand function. Is the economist's model refuted by the data in table 1.1?

Table 1.1
Global price and quantity of vitamin C, 1990 and 1994

Year	Price P_t \$/kg	Quantity Q_t (10^6 kg)
1990	12.42	4.11
1994	17.15	5.19

Source: Igami and Sugaya (2021)

Exercise 1.6. The economist in exercise 1.5 revises the model to hold that $Q_t = \exp^{\alpha+\beta t} P_t^{\epsilon}$, where α, β, and ϵ are scalar parameters, $\epsilon < 0$, and t is the calendar year. Is the revised model refuted by the data in table 1.1?

Exercise 1.7. Under the model in exercise 1.6, is the parameter $\theta = (\alpha, \beta, \epsilon)$ identified from data $Y = \{(P_t, Q_t)\}_{t=t',t''}$ for distinct years $t' \neq t''$?

Exercise 1.8. Now suppose the data $Y = \{(P_t, Q_t)\}_{t=t',t'',t'''}$ are for three distinct years $t' < t'' < t'''$. Give an example of conditions on the data under which the model in exercise 1.6 is refuted. Is the parameter $\theta = (\alpha, \beta, \epsilon)$ identified?

Exercise 1.9. Table 1.2 adds an additional year of data relative to table 1.1. Given the model in exercise 1.6, infer the parameter ϵ from the data in table 1.2.

Table 1.2
Global price and quantity of vitamin C, 1989, 1990, and 1994

Year	Price P_t \$/kg	Quantity Q_t (10^6 kg)
1989	12.64	3.44
1990	12.42	4.11
1994	17.15	5.19

Source: Igami and Sugaya (2021)

Exercise 1.10. In 1994 a significant portion of the market for vitamin C was controlled by a cartel (Connor, 2008; Igami and Sugaya, 2022). Suppose that in 1994 the cartel controlled the entire market and acted according to the static monopoly model, with a demand function given by the solution to exercise 1.9. What was the cartel's cost C_{1994} for producing a kilogram of vitamin C?

Exercise 1.11. Under the conditions of exercise 1.10, what would have been the gain in surplus from incrementally increasing the quantity of vitamin C in 1994?

Exercise 1.12. Under the conditions of exercise 1.10, what would have been the loss in profit to the cartel from reducing the price of vitamin C in 1994 to its 1990 price, leaving the cost of production, and the demand function, unchanged?

Exercise 1.13. Under the conditions of exercise 1.10, what would have been the gain in consumer surplus from reducing the price of vitamin C in 1994 to its 1990 price, leaving the demand function unchanged?

For the remaining exercises we'll introduce a new model. In this model, a dominant firm chooses a price $P^* > 0$. Rather than selling the full quantity demanded $Q^* = Q(P^*) > 0$, however, the dominant firm sells an amount given by $Q^* - F^*$, where $F^* = F(P)$ is an amount supplied by a competitive fringe of price-taking producers, whose output is determined by the strictly increasing and differentiable supply function $F : \mathbb{R}_{\geq 0} \to \mathbb{R}_{\geq 0}$. As in the monopoly model, we continue to suppose that the dominant firm has a constant marginal cost $C > 0$ of production.

Definition 1.6. The *dominant firm model* holds that

$$P^* \in \underset{P \in \mathbb{R}_{\geq 0}}{\arg\max} \left(Q(P) - F(P)\right)(P - C)$$
$$Q^* = Q\left(P^*\right)$$
$$F^* = F\left(P^*\right).$$

Exercise 1.14. Suppose that the dominant firm model holds and that $0 < F^* < Q^*$. Derive and interpret the first-order condition for optimal pricing by the dominant firm.

Exercise 1.15. As the cartel grew, so did the supply from a competitive fringe excluded from the cartel's arrangements. Table 1.3 includes information on the amount of vitamin C supplied by this competitive fringe. Suppose that $F(P) = F_0 P_t^{\phi}$ for $F_0 > 0$ a constant. What is the elasticity $\phi > 0$?

Table 1.3
Global price, total quantity, and fringe quantity of vitamin C, 1989, 1990, and 1994

Year	Price P_t \$/kg	Quantity Q_t (10^6 kg)	Fringe Supply F_t (10^6 kg)
1990	12.42	4.11	0.53
1994	17.15	5.19	1.66

Source: Igami and Sugaya (2021)

Exercise 1.16. Suppose that, in 1994, the dominant firm model held, with the cartel in the role of the dominant firm, the demand function given in exercise 1.6, and the fringe supply function given in exercise 1.15. What was the cartel's cost C_{1994} for producing a kilogram of vitamin C?

Exercise 1.17. Answer the questions in exercises 1.12 and 1.13 under the conditions of exercise 1.16.

Exercise 1.18. Under the conditions of exercise 1.16, what would have been the gain in total surplus from replacing all fringe production with cartel production in 1994, leaving the total quantity sold unchanged?

Notes

1. If not, then $\pi'\left(P^*\right) > 0$, a contradiction.

2. The total deadweight loss from monopoly is given by $\int_{Q^*}^{Q(C)} (P(Q) - C)\, dQ$ for $P(Q)$ the inverse demand function with $Q(P(Q)) = Q$. The expression in equation (1.2) then follows by the fundamental theorem of calculus.

2

Entry

Each agent that enters a market pays a cost $F > 0$. If N agents enter the market, each entrant gets an expected payoff of V/N where $V > 0$ is the value of some fixed resource. For example, the agents could be risk-neutral construction companies that have to pay a cost F to enter a government procurement lottery with a fixed value V and a uniform probability $1/N$ of allocation to each entrant. Or the agents could be risk-neutral political candidates that pay a cost F to enter an election contest, with a value V of winning the election and a uniform probability $1/N$ of winning for each entrant. Or the agents could be firms that have to pay a cost F to enter a market where a fixed set of customers will be allocated evenly among the entrants (see exercise 2.4).

A natural solution concept holds that the equilibrium number of entrants is such that all entrants profit from entry, but a further entrant would not.

Definition 2.1. The *fixed-pie entry model* holds that

$$\frac{V}{N^* + 1} < F \leq \frac{V}{N^*}, \tag{2.1}$$

where $V, F > 0$, $N^* \in \mathbb{N}$, and we may take $V/0 = \infty$.

The pattern of inequalities in equation (2.1) encodes a simplifying refinement that agents enter when indifferent.

2.1 Data from a Single Market

From data $\{F, V, N^*\}$ we can refute the fixed-pie entry model if equation (2.1) fails. More interesting is the case where the data include only two of these three objects.

Question 2.1. *Consider each of the following cases:*

- *The data are* $\{F, V\}$, *and* N^* *is not directly observed.*
- *The data are* $\{V, N^*\}$, *and* F *is not directly observed.*
- *The data are* $\{F, N^*\}$, *and* V *is not directly observed.*

In each case, consider:

- *When (if ever) can we refute the fixed-pie entry model?*
- *What (if anything) can we say about the unobserved element of* $\{F, V, N^*\}$*?*

Pause to reflect. Write down your answer before continuing.

Consider first the case where the data are $\{F, V\}$, and N^* is not directly observed. Any $F, V > 0$ are, by definition, consistent with the fixed-pie entry model, so the model is not refuted if these values are strictly positive and is trivially refuted otherwise. Exercise 2.1 proves that equation (2.1) defines a unique $N^* \in \mathbb{N}$, from which it follows that N^* is identified in this case.

Consider next the case in which the data are $\{V, N^*\}$ and F is not directly observed. Exercise 2.2 proves that whenever $N^* \in \mathbb{N}$ and $V > 0$, there is some $F > 0$ satisfying equation (2.1), from which it follows that the model is not refuted if $N^* \in \mathbb{N}$ and $V > 0$, and is trivially refuted otherwise.

It is also clear that F is not identified. Suppose, for example, that $N^* = 0$ and $V = 1$. Then F may, for example, be 2, or it may be 3. Notice, however, that in this case F may *not* be 0.75, because if it were, an agent would find it attractive to enter, and in particular we would have that $N^* = 1$ following equation (2.1). Thus, while we cannot identify F, we *can* use the data to say something about its value. To express this situation requires additional terminology.

Definition 2.2. Consider a model that, given primitives Ξ, specifies a set $\mathcal{Y}(\Xi)$ of admissible values of some observed data, and a value $\theta(\Xi)$ of some parameter. For any realization Y^*, let

$$\Theta\left(Y^*\right) = \cup_{\{\Xi : Y^* \in \mathcal{Y}(\Xi)\}} \{\theta(\Xi)\}$$

be the *identified set* for θ, i.e., the set of values of θ consistent with realization Y^*, where we may take $\Theta(Y^*) = \emptyset$ if Y^* refutes the model. Now say that the parameter θ is *partially identified* if $\Theta(Y^*) \neq \Theta(Y^{**})$ for some Y^*, Y^{**} such that $\Theta(Y^*), \Theta(Y^{**}) \neq \emptyset$.

Exercise 2.3 proves a sense in which partial identification is a weaker property than identification.

We can now say the following.

Fact 2.1. Under the fixed-pie entry model with data $Y^* = \{V, N^*\}$, with $N^* \in \mathbb{N}$ and $V > 0$, the identified set for F is

$$\mathcal{F}\left(N^*, V\right) = \left(\frac{V}{N^*+1}, \frac{V}{N^*}\right]$$

and F is partially identified.

A similar conclusion holds when the data are $\{F, N^*\}$, and that case is left to the interested reader.

Fact 2.1 is useful because it allows us to place bounds on the cost of entry based only on knowledge of the size of the "pie" and the number of entrants. (See exercise 2.4.) Bounds on costs may be useful, for example, to assess the resource cost of excess entry in a market. (See exercise 2.5.) Fact 2.1 illustrates principle 2 as well as the following principle.

Principle 3. *A useful economic model might only tell us a range of values for what we want to know.*

Exercises

Exercise 2.1. There is exactly one value $N^* \in \mathbb{N}$ that solves equation (2.1) when $F, V > 0$. Prove this.

Exercise 2.2. There is some $F > 0$ that satisfies equation (2.1) when $N^* \in \mathbb{N}$ and $V > 0$. Prove this.

Exercise 2.3. If, under some model, the parameter θ can take on more than one value and is identified, then θ is partially identified. Prove this.

Exercise 2.4. Table 2.1 shows the number of listeners and number of stations in each of three formats in the Providence radio market in 2000. The table also shows the total listeners and total advertising revenue across all formats. Assume that each station's advertising revenue is proportional to its number of listeners. Assume that each format has a fixed number of listeners who are indifferent to which station they listen to, and therefore pick stations uniformly at random from among the available ones (Steiner 1952). Assume that each format is a distinct market characterized by the fixed-pie entry model. What is the identified set for F in each format?

Exercise 2.5. Because listeners are indifferent among different stations within a format, a policymaker considers restricting licensing of radio stations so that only one station in each format may operate in the market. Under the model in exercise 2.4 and the data in

Table 2.1
Listeners and revenue in the Providence radio market in spring 2000

Format	Listeners	Stations N^*	Revenue
Contemporary hit radio	19,000	2	—
Talk	19,700	4	—
Modern rock	12,200	2	—
Total	145,800	22	48,300,000

Source: Sanders (2001)
Notes: Listeners is the number of listeners across all stations in an average quarter-hour time slot. Revenue is annual in dollars. Total includes formats other than those listed.

table 2.1, what is the identified set for the cost savings from such a policy, separately for each format? What is the identified set for the total savings when applied to all of the listed formats?

Exercise 2.6. Suppose the policymaker in exercise 2.5 can only impose the restrictive licensing policy on one of the listed formats. Which format should the policymaker choose in order to achieve the greatest cost savings, or can you not tell?

Exercise 2.7. In a stylized version of the EuroMillions (2022) lottery, each of the N^* risk-neutral players pays a fee of $F = €2.50$ for a chance at winning the prize V, which is determined as half of the receipts, $V = 0.5FN^*$. If the other assumptions of the fixed-pie entry model hold, what is N^*?

Exercise 2.8. These days a typical EuroMillions prize is around $V = €60$ million (EuroMillions 2022). Imagine that in addition to paying the cost $F > 0$, entrants obtain a benefit $B \geq 0$ because it is fun to play, so that the equilibrium condition is now

$$\frac{V}{N^* + 1} < F - B \leq \frac{V}{N^*}.$$

If the other details follow exercise 2.7, what can you say about the value of B?

Exercise 2.9. Continuing with the setting of exercise 2.8, suppose that $B = 0$ but that, for N^* sufficiently large, potential entrants overestimate the probability of winning by a factor of $\gamma \geq 1$, so that equilibrium with large N^* requires

$$\gamma \frac{V}{N^* + 1} < F \leq \gamma \frac{V}{N^*}.$$

What can you say about the value of γ?

Exercise 2.10. Combining the settings of exercises 2.8 and 2.9, suppose that entrants may obtain a benefit from playing and potential entrants may also overestimate the probability of winning, so that the equilibrium condition is now

$$\gamma \frac{V}{N^* + 1} < F - B \leq \gamma \frac{V}{N^*}.$$

What can you say about the values of B and γ?

2.2 Data from a Set of Markets

Imagine that we have data $\left\{\left(V_t, N_t^*\right)\right\}_{t=1}^{T}$ from a set of markets t. The markets may be the same geographic market at different points in time, or they may be different geographic markets, or different market niches in the same place and time.

What can we learn from looking at a set of markets as a group rather than a single market in isolation? To make the question more concrete, consider figure 2.1, which is based on data from the Boston radio market, similar to the data from the Providence radio market that you saw in exercise 2.4. The figure shows a scatterplot, across formats t, of the number of stations N_t^* against the revenue per station V/N_t^*.

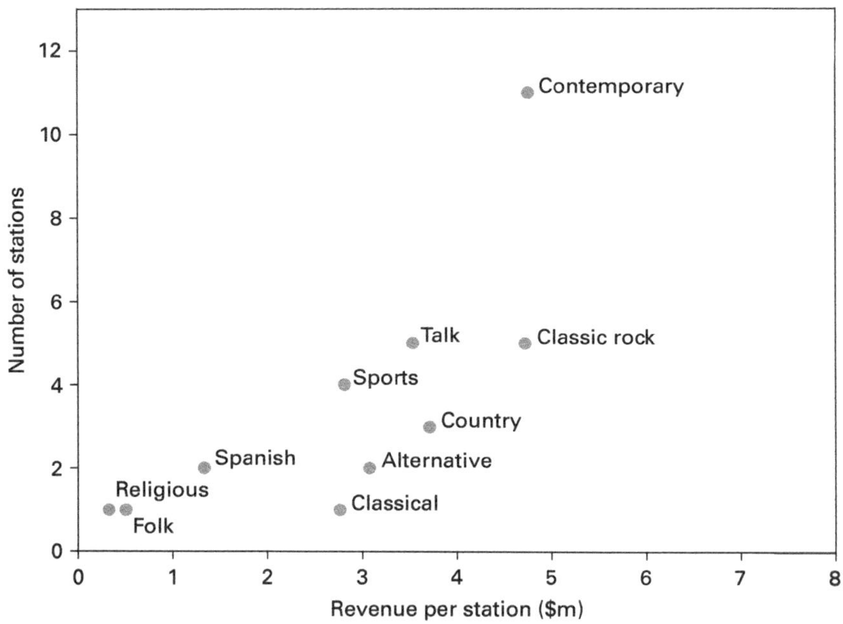

Figure 2.1
Number of stations and mean station revenue by format in the Boston radio market

Notes: The unit of observation is a format. The y-axis shows the number of stations operating in the format in 2022. The x-axis shows the estimated revenue per station in 2022 among stations in the format. The number of stations operating in the format comes from RadioInsight (2022), where for simplicity some formats are aggregated together. The estimated revenue per station is calculated assuming that a format's revenue is proportional to the total cumes of its stations, and that per-capita radio revenue in Boston is equal to the national value from BIA Advisory Services (2021), interpolated linearly between their 2020 and 2025 estimates.

Question 2.2. *What are the key patterns in figure 2.1? Are these patterns supportive of the fixed-pie entry model?*

Pause to reflect. Write down your answer before continuing.

From the standpoint of the fixed-pie entry model, figure 2.1 may seem to present a mixed picture. On the one hand, the figure shows evidence of a positive association between the number of stations in a format, N_t^*, and the revenue per station, V_t/N_t^*, consistent with the idea that revenue drives entry into the market. On the other hand, figure 2.1 shows that one format (e.g., country) can have fewer stations than another format (e.g., talk) despite having higher revenue per station, which might suggest other forces at play.

Toward a more formal analysis, recall that definition 2.1 specifies equilibrium in a given market. To apply the fixed-pie entry model to figure 2.1, we must first say how we will apply definition 2.1 to a set of markets. The following definition specifies some candidate approaches.

Definition 2.3. The *homogeneous fixed-pie entry model* holds that the fixed-pie entry model applies in each market $t \in \{1, \ldots, T\}$ with primitives $\Xi_t = \Xi = (F, V) \in \mathbb{R}^2_{>0}$ for all t.

The *partially homogeneous fixed-pie entry model* holds that the fixed-pie entry model applies in each market $t \in \{1, \ldots, T\}$ with primitives $\Xi_t = (F, V_t) \in \mathbb{R}^2_{>0}$ for all t.

The *heterogeneous fixed-pie entry model* holds that the the fixed-pie entry model applies in each market $t \in \{1, \ldots, T\}$ with primitives $\Xi_t = (F_t, V_t) \in \mathbb{R}^2_{>0}$ for all t.

The models in definition 2.3 differ in whether, and in what way, they restrict variation in the primitives across markets. The homogeneous model holds that primitives are identical in all markets, the partially homogeneous model that only the value V_t may vary across markets, and the heterogeneous model that both the fixed cost F_t and the value V_t may vary across markets.

Question 2.3. *Which, if any, of the models in definition 2.3 is refuted by figure 2.1?*

Pause to reflect. Write down your answer before continuing.

The homogeneous and heterogeneous models are simplest. The homogeneous model is refuted by figure 2.1 because we can readily verify that there are markets t, t' such that $V_t \neq V_{t'}$. The heterogeneous model is not refuted by figure 2.1 because the reasoning in exercise 2.2 implies that the fixed-pie entry model is not refuted by any data $\{(N_t^*, V_t)\}_{t=1}^T$ such that $N_t^* \in \mathbb{N}$ and $V_t > 0$ for all $t \in \{1, \ldots, T\}$.

The partially homogeneous model is more interesting. It is also refuted by figure 2.1. To see why, observe that by equation (2.1), under the partially homogeneous model we must have that $F \in \cap_{t=1}^T \left(\frac{V_t}{N_t^*+1}, \frac{V_t}{N_t^*}\right]$. Figure 2.2 depicts the interval $\left(\frac{V_t}{N_t^*+1}, \frac{V_t}{N_t^*}\right]$ for each market t based on the data in figure 2.1. Because we cannot draw a single vertical line that passes through all of the depicted intervals, we know that $\cap_{t=1}^T \left(\frac{V_t}{N_t^*+1}, \frac{V_t}{N_t^*}\right] = \emptyset$, and thus that the partially homogeneous model is refuted.

Definition 2.4. Consider a model that, given primitives Ξ, specifies a set $\mathcal{Y}(\Xi)$ of admissible values of some observed data. An element of Ξ is an *observed primitive* if it

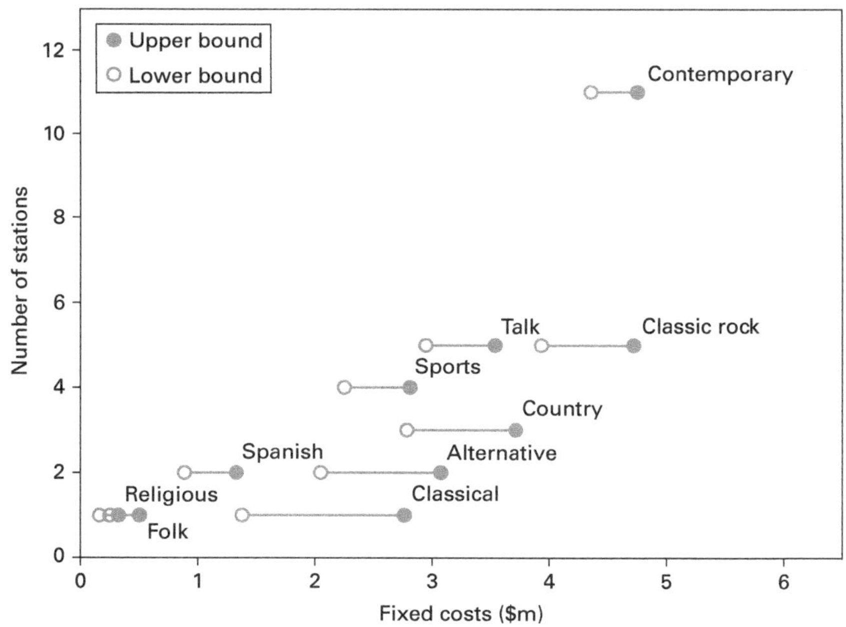

Figure 2.2
Number of stations and implied range of fixed costs by format in the Boston radio market

Notes: The unit of observation is a format. The y-axis shows the number of stations operating in the format. The line segments show the identified set of fixed costs under the heterogeneous fixed-pie entry model. Details of data construction follow figure 2.1.

is an element of a realization $Y^* \in \mathcal{Y}(\Xi)$ of the data, and an *unobserved primitive* if it is not. An element of a realization $Y^* \in \mathcal{Y}(\Xi)$ is an *observed outcome* if it is not a primitive.

An unobserved primitive may be identified or partially identified, but it is not directly observed.

Unobserved economic primitives play an important role in quantitative economics, as suggested by figure 2.2.

Principle 4. *Models without variation in unobserved economic primitives are typically refuted by economic data.*

To see principle 4 at work, consider the following question.

Question 2.4. *How would figure 2.1 look if outcomes were consistent with the partially homogeneous fixed-pie entry model?*

Pause to reflect. Write down your answer before continuing.

Figure 2.3 depicts a hypothetical version of figure 2.1 for the situation in which we take V_t as given from the data and take F as the midpoint of the interval $\left(\frac{V_t}{N_t^*+1}, \frac{V_t}{N_t^*}\right]$ for one of the formats t.

The patterns in figure 2.3 differ from those in figure 2.1 in at least two important respects. First, unlike figure 2.1, figure 2.3 does not show evidence of a positive association between the number of stations N_t^* in a given format t and the revenue per station V_t/N_t^* in the format, and may even suggest a negative association. Second, relative to figure 2.1, figure 2.3 shows much less dispersion in the revenue per station V_t/N_t^* across formats t.

To build an intuition for the patterns in figure 2.3, fix F and consider the situation in which V_t is large for all formats, so that N_t^* is also large, and hence $\frac{N_t^*}{N_t^*+1} \approx 1$. In this case, we may loosely think that $\frac{V_t}{N_t^*} \approx \frac{V_t}{N_t^*+1}$, so under the partially homogeneous model $F \approx \frac{V_t}{N_t^*}$

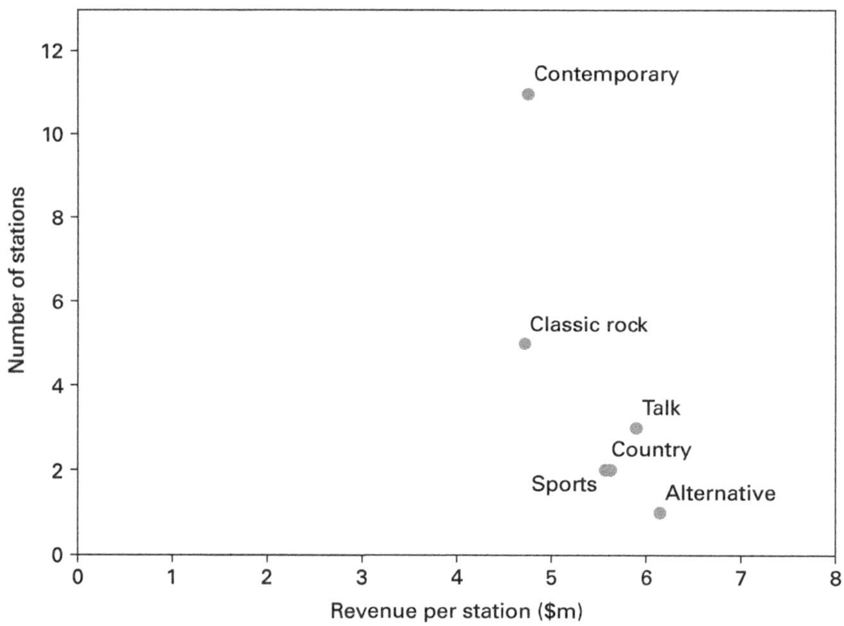

Figure 2.3
Number of stations and mean station revenue by format in the Boston radio market, counterfactual scenario under the partially homogeneous fixed-pie entry model

Notes: The unit of observation is a format. The y-axis shows the number of stations operating in the format. The x-axis shows the revenue per station in the segment. The total revenue in each format is assumed to be as calculated for figure 2.1. The fixed cost of entry in each format is assumed to be at the midpoint of the interval depicted in figure 2.2 for the contemporary format. The number of stations in each format is calculated according to the partially homogeneous fixed-pie entry model given the assumed revenue and fixed cost of entry. Formats for which the number of stations is zero are omitted from the plot.

for all t. Therefore, under the partially homogeneous model, a scatterplot of the number of stations N_t^* against the revenue per station $\frac{V_t}{N_t^*}$ will lie approximately along a vertical line, more akin to figure 2.3 than to figure 2.1. In this case, then, principle 4 applies in a very strong sense: absent variation in the unobserved primitive F_t, the observed primitive V_t must be approximately proportional to the observed outcome N_t^*, which is clearly contradicted by the data.

In summary, we have that figure 2.1 refutes the homogeneous model (because V_t varies across formats t), refutes the partially homogeneous model (loosely, because $\frac{V_t}{N_t^*}$ varies too much across formats t), and does not refute the heterogeneous model (because that model can accommodate essentially any pattern). Returning to question 2.2, where do these conclusions leave us regarding the applicability of the fixed-pie entry model to the data in figure 2.1? Contrasting the partially homogeneous model to the heterogeneous model suggests that the answer turns, in part, on whether the variation in the unobserved economic primitive F_t necessary to rationalize the data in figure 2.1 is plausible.

Figure 2.2 implies, for example, that a contemporary station costs at least \$1.28 million more per year to operate than an alternative station, and that a classic rock station costs at least \$0.86 million more per year to operate than an alternative station. If there are economic reasons to find such differences plausible, for example differences in staffing or music licensing costs, then we may find figure 2.1 supportive of the heterogeneous fixed-pie entry model. If there are no economic reasons to find such differences plausible, for example because all music stations have similar operating costs, then we may find figure 2.1 unsupportive of the heterogeneous fixed-pie entry model. Either way, we have illustrated another important principle of quantitative economics.

Principle 5. *Unobserved economic primitives are economic variables and are therefore subject to economic reasoning.*

Exercises

Exercise 2.11. Table 2.2 gives the data underlying figure 2.1. Under the heterogeneous fixed-pie entry model, what is the association between the identified set for F_t and the value V_t across formats t? What economic interpretation can you give this pattern?

Exercise 2.12. Suppose that the values for total revenue given in table 2.2 are mismeasured, so that the data are $\left\{\left(N_t^*, \hat{V}_t\right)\right\}_{t=1}^T$ for $\hat{V}_t$ the reported total revenue in format t and V_t the true revenue in format t. Under this assumption about measurement, which, if any, of the models in definition 2.3 is refuted by the data $\left\{\left(N_t^*, \hat{V}_t\right)\right\}_{t=1}^T$ in table 2.2?

Table 2.2
Number of stations and total revenue by format in the Boston radio market

Format t	Number of stations N_t^*	Total revenue (million \$) V_t
Contemporary	11	52.29
Classic rock	5	23.60
Talk	5	17.68
Sports	4	11.25
Country	3	11.14
Alternative	2	6.15
Classical	1	2.76
Spanish	2	2.66
Religious	1	0.33
Folk	1	0.51

Notes: Details of data construction follow figure 2.1.

Exercise 2.13. Let $\theta = \max_{t\in\{1,\ldots,T\}} \left|\hat{V}_t - V_t\right|$ denote the largest measurement error across all formats. Under the partially homogeneous model and the assumption about measurement introduced in exercise 2.12, what is the smallest element of the identified set for θ if we consider only the contemporary and classic rock formats in table 2.2? What if we consider only the talk and classic rock formats in table 2.2?

Exercise 2.14. Under the assumption about measurement error introduced in exercise 2.12 and the definition introduced in exercise 2.13, let $\Theta(Y^*)$ be the identified set for θ under the partially homogeneous model with the data Y^* given in table 2.2. Now let $\Theta\left(Y^*_{-\tau}\right)$ be the identified set for θ under the partially homogeneous model with the data $Y^*_{-\tau}$ formed by removing one format τ from table 2.2. Then $\min\Theta\left(Y^*_{-\tau}\right) \leq \min\Theta(Y^*)$. Prove this.

3

Demand

In each market $t \in \{1, \ldots, T\}$, a quantity $Q_t \geq 0$ of a good is sold to a population of consumers at a price $P_t \geq 0$. The markets could be time periods (e.g., years) and the good an agricultural commodity (e.g., wheat) that is traded on a world market. Or the markets could be geographic locations (e.g., cities) and the good a commodity (e.g., concrete) that is produced and sold locally. Or the markets could be combinations of these: a particular location at a particular point in time.

Definition 3.1. The *homogeneous demand model* holds that $Q_t = Q(P_t)$ for $Q : \mathbb{R}_{\geq 0} \to \mathbb{R}_{\geq 0}$ a strictly decreasing function.

> **Question 3.1.** *From data* $\{(P_t, Q_t)\}_{t=1}^{T} \in \mathbb{R}_{\geq 0}^{T}$, *can we ever refute the homogeneous demand model? If so, when?*
>
> *Pause to reflect. Write down your answer before continuing.*

3.1 Data from Two Markets

Figure 3.1 gives an example of a dataset that refutes the homogeneous demand model. It features $T = 2$ markets, with $(P_2, Q_2) > (P_1, Q_1)$. No strictly decreasing function $Q(\cdot)$ can simultaneously satisfy $Q_2 = Q(P_2)$ and $Q_1 = Q(P_1)$.

Figure 3.1 illustrates the following fact.

Fact 3.1. From data $\{(P_t, Q_t)\}_{t=1}^{T} \in \mathbb{R}_{\geq 0}^{T}$, we can refute the homogeneous demand model if and only if there exist $t', t'' \in \{1, ..., T\}$ such that either (i) $P_{t''} \geq P_{t'}$ and $Q_{t''} > Q_{t'}$ or (ii) $P_{t''} > P_{t'}$ and $Q_{t''} \geq Q_{t'}$.

Exercise 3.1 proves fact 3.1. Fact 3.1 illustrates principle 4: we will rarely be able to explain data from a set of markets if we assume that all markets share a single demand function.

A more realistic model holds that demand functions differ across markets, for example because preferences differ.

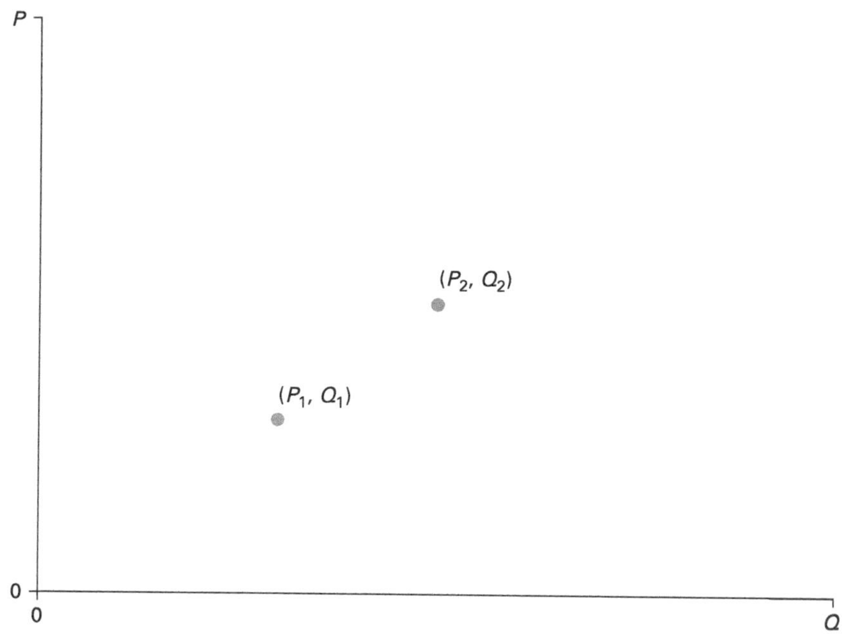

Figure 3.1
An example dataset that refutes the homogeneous demand model

Notes: The plot shows an example of a dataset with $T = 2$ and $(P_2, Q_2) > (P_1, Q_1)$, such that the homogeneous demand model is refuted.

Definition 3.2. The *heterogeneous demand model* holds that $Q_t = Q_t(P_t)$ for $Q_t : \mathbb{R}_{\geq 0} \to \mathbb{R}_{\geq 0}$ a strictly decreasing function for each $t \in \{1, \ldots, T\}$.

In contrast to the homogeneous demand model, the heterogeneous demand model is not refutable from data $\{(P_t, Q_t)\}_{t=1}^{T} \in \mathbb{R}_{\geq 0}^{T}$.

Fact 3.2. From data $\{(P_t, Q_t)\}_{t=1}^{T} \in \mathbb{R}_{\geq 0}^{T}$, we cannot refute the heterogeneous demand model.

Exercise 3.2 proves fact 3.2 constructively.

Fact 3.2 implies that the data in figure 3.1 do not refute the heterogeneous demand model. It may therefore be interesting to ask what we can learn about the demand functions $Q_1(\cdot)$ and $Q_2(\cdot)$ from the data in figure 3.1.

Question 3.2. *From the data $\{(P_t, Q_t)\}_{t=1}^{2} \in \mathbb{R}_{\geq 0}^{T}$ in figure 3.1, can we say anything about the difference in the demand functions $Q_2(\cdot)$and $Q_1(\cdot)$ under the heterogeneous demand model?*

Pause to reflect. Write down your answer before continuing.

There are many ways to measure the difference between two demand functions. To fix ideas, consider the parameter $\Delta = Q_2(P_1) - Q_1(P_1)$, which measures the difference in the quantity demanded between markets 1 and 2 at the price P_1 that prevails in market 1. In the context of figure 3.1, Δ is the horizontal distance between $Q_2(\cdot)$ and $Q_1(\cdot)$ measured at $P = P_1$, drawn in figure 3.2 for a hypothetical pair of demand functions $Q_2(\cdot), Q_1(\cdot)$.

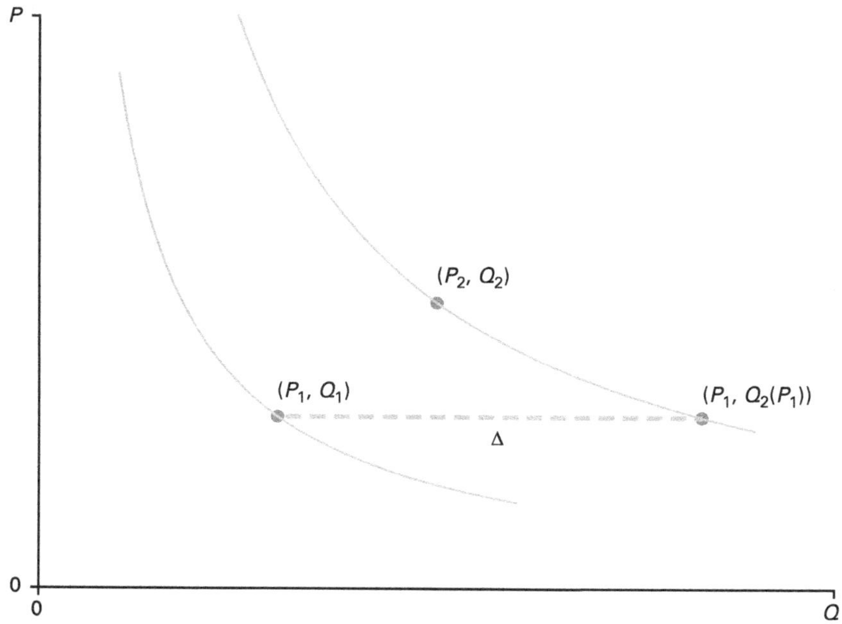

Figure 3.2
Measuring the difference between two demand functions

Notes: The plot depicts the dataset in figure 3.1 along with data-consistent demand functions $Q_1(\cdot), Q_2(\cdot)$. The parameter $\Delta = Q_2(P_1) - Q_1(P_1)$ measures the horizontal distance between the functions at price $P = P_1$.

Question 3.3. *Given the data $\{(P_t, Q_t)\}_{t=1}^{2} \in \mathbb{R}^T_{\geq 0}$ in figure 3.1, what is the identified set for $\Delta = Q_2(P_1) - Q_1(P_1)$ under the heterogeneous demand model?*

Pause to reflect. Write down your answer before continuing.

It may be tempting to conclude that the identified set for Δ is $\mathbb{R}$, i.e. that we can learn nothing about Δ from the data in figure 3.1. One way to see that this is not the case is to pick a value of Δ and attempt to draw demand functions $Q_2(\cdot), Q_1(\cdot)$ that are consistent with it.

Start with $\Delta = 0$. In this case we have that $Q_2(P_1) = Q_1(P_1)$, which implies that $Q_2(\cdot)$ is not strictly decreasing since $P_2 > P_1$ and $Q_2 = Q_2(P_2) > Q_1(P_1) = Q_1$. A similar contradiction arises for any $\Delta \leq Q_2 - Q_1$.

Fact 3.3. Given data $\{(P_t, Q_t)\}_{t=1}^{2}$ with $(P_2, Q_2) > (P_1, Q_1) \geq (0, 0)$, the identified set for $\Delta = Q_2(P_1) - Q_1(P_1)$ under the heterogeneous demand model is $(Q_2 - Q_1, \infty)$.

Exercise 3.3 proves fact 3.3.

Intuitively, because demand is decreasing in price, and P_2 is greater than P_1, whatever difference in quantity we observe between markets 1 and 2 must be smaller than what would have obtained, counterfactually, had prices been identical between the two markets. We can extend this logic quantitatively.

Let $\overline{\varepsilon} = \frac{Q_2(P_2) - Q_2(P_1)}{P_2 - P_1} < 0$ be the average slope of the demand curve $Q_2(\cdot)$ between prices P_1 and P_2. The parameter $\overline{\varepsilon}$, illustrated in figure 3.3, describes how quickly demand falls, on average, as the price rises between P_1 and P_2 in market 2. No matter what the shape of $Q_2(\cdot)$, $\overline{\varepsilon}$ is well-defined as long as $P_2 \neq P_1$. If $Q_2(\cdot)$ is differentiable, then by the mean value theorem $\overline{\varepsilon}$ corresponds to the exact slope of $Q_2(\cdot)$ somewhere between P_1 and P_2.[1] If Q and P are natural logarithms of quantity and price, respectively, then $\overline{\varepsilon}$ may be thought of as an average elasticity.

By the definition of $\Delta = Q_2(P_1) - Q_1(P_1)$ we can write that

$$(Q_2 - Q_1) = \Delta + \overline{\varepsilon}(P_2 - P_1). \tag{3.1}$$

In words, the difference in the quantity sold between markets 1 and 2 is comprised of a difference in the the quantity demanded at a fixed price and a substitution response to the difference in prices between the markets. These two terms correspond to the two dashed line segments in figure 3.3.

The parameter $(\Delta, \overline{\varepsilon})$ is useful for many purposes. By equation (3.1), an economist who knows the parameter $(\Delta, \overline{\varepsilon})$ can predict the difference in quantities $Q_2 - Q_1$ from the difference in price $P_2 - P_1$ without knowing any other properties of the demand functions $Q_1(\cdot), Q_2(\cdot)$. As we saw in chapter 1, knowledge of the elasticity of demand, which is closely related to $\overline{\varepsilon}$, can be useful for inferring a monopolist's costs and the welfare effects of factual and counterfactual changes in the market price. Knowledge of Δ, in turn, may be useful if we wish to study the determinants of demand, for example the effect of differences across markets in income or other consumer characteristics. Unfortunately, absent further information, not much more can be said about the parameter $(\Delta, \overline{\varepsilon})$.

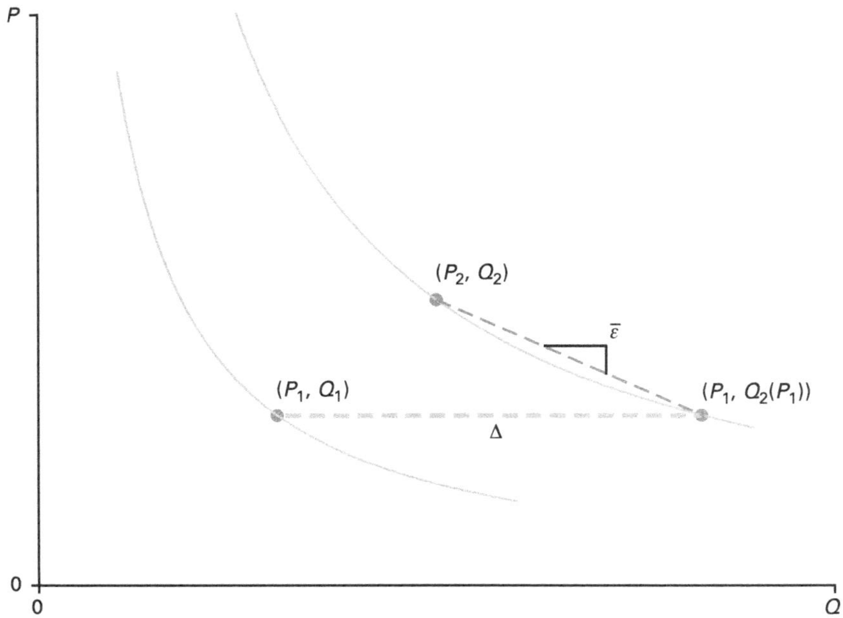

Figure 3.3
Measuring the slope of a demand function

Notes: The plot depicts the dataset in figure 3.1 along with data-consistent demand functions $Q_1(\cdot), Q_2(\cdot)$. The parameter $\Delta = Q_2(P_1) - Q_1(P_1)$ measures the horizontal distance between the functions at price $P = P_1$. The parameter $\overline{\varepsilon} = \frac{Q_2(P_2)-Q_2(P_1)}{P_2-P_1}$ measures the average slope of the demand curve $Q_2(\cdot)$ between prices P_1 and P_2.

Fact 3.4. Given data $\{(P_t, Q_t)\}_{t=1}^{2}$ with $(P_2, Q_2) > (P_1, Q_1) \geq (0,0)$, the identified set for $(\Delta, \overline{\varepsilon})$ under the heterogeneous demand model is $\left\{\left(d, \frac{Q_2-Q_1-d}{P_2-P_1}\right) : d > Q_2 - Q_1\right\}$. Accordingly, the identified set for $\overline{\varepsilon}$ is $(-\infty, 0)$.

Fact 3.4 follows from the same reasoning as fact 3.3 given the identitiy in equation (3.1).

3.2 Data from Three Markets

One route to learning $(\Delta, \overline{\varepsilon})$ is to envision that we have a third market that shares the same demand function as one of the other two.

Definition 3.3. The *partially homogeneous demand model* holds that $Q_t = Q_t(P_t)$ for $Q: \mathbb{R}_{\geq 0} \to \mathbb{R}_{\geq 0}$ a strictly decreasing function, with $Q_{t'}(\cdot) = Q_{t''}(\cdot)$ for all $t', t'' \in \mathcal{T} \subset \{1, ..., T\}$, with $1 < |\mathcal{T}| < T$ and $\mathcal{T}$ known.

In words, the partially homogeneous demand model holds that the demand function is heterogeneous except on some known subset of markets $\mathcal{T}$. If the markets t represent different periods of time, the partially homogeneous model could reflect a situation in which preferences are believed to have been stable between certain periods. If the markets t represent different geographic markets, the partially homogeneous model could reflect a situation in which certain markets are believed to have demographically similar consumers.

From the standpoint of learning $(\Delta, \overline{\varepsilon})$, an especially convenient situation is the one depicted in figure 3.4, in which a third market, $t = 3$, shares the demand function of market 2 and the prevailing price of market 1.

Figure 3.4 proves the following.

Fact 3.5. Given data $\{(P_t, Q_t)\}_{t=1}^{3}$ with $(P_2, Q_2) > (P_1, Q_1) \geq (0,0)$ and $P_3 = P_1$, the parameter $(\Delta, \overline{\varepsilon})$ is identified under the partially homogeneous demand model with $\mathcal{T} = \{2, 3\}$.

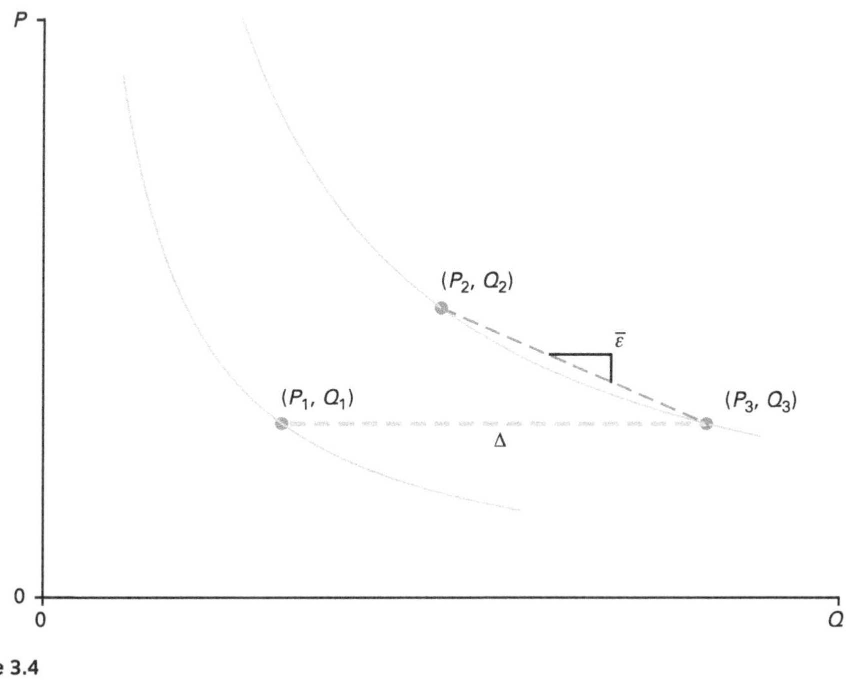

Figure 3.4
A convenient third data point

Notes: The plot augments the one in figure 3.3 with data from a third market, $t = 3$, that shares the same demand function as the second market, $Q_3(\cdot) = Q_2(\cdot)$. The price P_3 in the third market is identical to the price P_1 in the first market, permitting identification of $(\Delta, \overline{\varepsilon})$.

Fact 3.5 is useful for clarifying the conditions for identification of $(\Delta, \overline{\varepsilon})$. But on its own it is not of much practical use. For one thing, we are unlikely to find two markets that are known to share literally identical demand functions. For another, even if we were in such a fortunate situation, it seems unlikely that we would observe the exact same price rise in two distinct markets.

To illustrate the importance of the second point, consider what would happen if P_3 were a bit below P_1, as in figure 3.5.

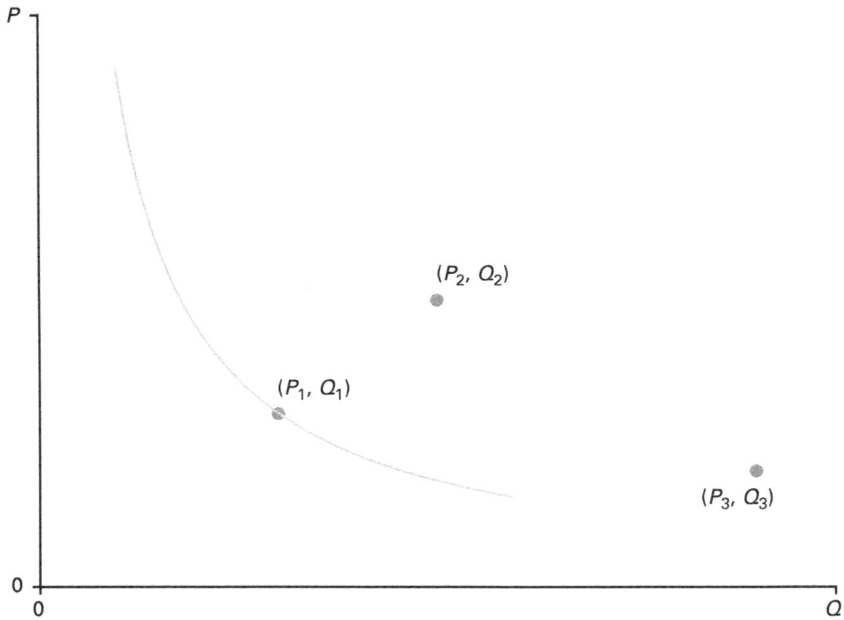

Figure 3.5
A less convenient third data point

Notes: In contrast to figure 3.4, the price P_3 in market $t = 3$ is here strictly below the price P_1 in market $t = 1$. As a result, $(\Delta, \overline{\varepsilon})$ is not identified.

> **Question 3.4.** *Given the data* $\{(P_t, Q_t)\}_{t=1}^{3} \in \mathbb{R}_{\geq 0}^{T}$ *in figure 3.5, what is the identified set for* $\Delta = Q_2(P_1) - Q_1(P_1)$ *under the partially homogeneous demand model with* $\mathcal{T} = \{2, 3\}$*?*
>
> *Pause to reflect. Write down your answer before continuing.*

Geometrically, the fact that the demand function $Q_2(\cdot)$ is strictly decreasing means that $Q_3 = Q_2(P_3) > Q_2(P_1) > Q_2(P_2) = Q_2$. We can therefore say that

$$\Delta = Q_2(P_1) - Q_1(P_1) < Q_2(P_3) - Q_1(P_1) = Q_3 - Q_1.$$

In fact, this is the only additional restriction on Δ that comes from the inclusion of the third data point (P_3, Q_3).

Fact 3.6. Given data $\{(P_t, Q_t)\}_{t=1}^{3} \in \mathbb{R}_{\geq 0}^{3}$ with $(P_2, Q_2) > (P_1, Q_1)$, $P_3 < P_1$, and $Q_3 > Q_2$, the identified set for $\Delta = Q_2(P_1) - Q_1(P_1)$ under the partially homogeneous demand model with $\mathcal{T} = \{2, 3\}$ is $(Q_2 - Q_1, Q_3 - Q_1)$.

Exercise 3.4 proves fact 3.6.

It may be surprising that the identified set for Δ in the setting of figure 3.5 does not depend at all on the value of P_3. After all, when $P_3 = P_1$, we know from fact 3.5 that Δ is identified. Yet, according to fact 3.6, when $P_3 < P_1$, we cannot identify Δ even when P_3 is arbitrarily close to P_1.

Figure 3.6 illustrates why. The figure shows two strictly decreasing demand functions $Q_2(\cdot)$ that pass through the points (P_2, Q_2) and (P_3, Q_3) and are therefore consistent with the partially homogeneous demand model. These functions take very different paths between (P_2, Q_2) and (P_3, Q_3), and accordingly imply very different values of Δ, close to the boundaries of the identified set. Similar paths can be drawn even when P_3 is arbitrarily close to P_1.

Figure 3.6 illustrates that learning Δ is a problem of interpolating an unknown function. If all we know about this function is that it is strictly decreasing, the range of possible interpolations is substantial. If, instead, we are able to use economic theory or intuition to impose further restrictions on the demand function, then we may be able to narrow the range of possible interpolations considerably. For example, it is clear from figure 3.6 that if $Q_2(\cdot)$ is known to be linear on (P_2, P_3), then $(\Delta, \overline{\varepsilon})$ is identified.

Principle 6. *With finite data, restrictions on functional form can be valuable, and even essential, for learning what we want to know.*

Of course, restrictions on functional form need not be as specific as linearity. For example, we might be prepared to relax linearity but otherwise bound the curvature or "wiggliness" of the demand function.

Exercises

Exercise 3.1. Prove fact 3.1.

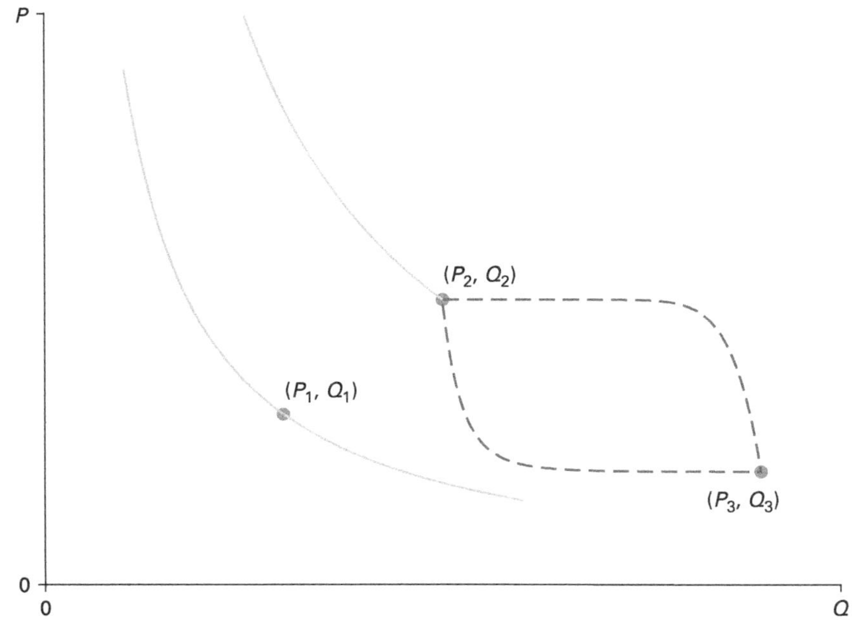

Figure 3.6
Illustrating the identified set for Δ

Notes: In the setting of figure 3.5, the plot illustrates two demand functions $Q_2(\cdot)$ that are each consistent with the data and with the partially homogeneous demand model. The two demand functions imply very different values of Δ, close to the boundaries of the identified set $(Q_2 - Q_1, Q_3 - Q_1)$.

Exercise 3.2. Prove fact 3.2 constructively, i.e., by giving an example of a set of strictly decreasing functions $Q_t : \mathbb{R}_{\geq 0} \rightarrow \mathbb{R}_{\geq 0}$ such that $Q_t = Q_t(P_t)$ for all $t \in \{1, ..., T\}$.

Exercise 3.3. Prove fact 3.3.

Exercise 3.4. Prove fact 3.6.

Exercise 3.5. In the setting of fact 3.6, what is the identified set for $\overline{\varepsilon}$?

Definition 3.4. The *isoelastic heterogeneous demand model* is a special case of the heterogeneous demand model with $Q_t(P) = \overline{Q}_t P^{\varepsilon}$ for all $t \in \{1, ..., T\}$, where $\overline{Q}_t > 0$ is a market-specific constant and $\varepsilon < 0$ is an elasticity.

Exercise 3.6. Table 3.1 gives annual data on the world price and consumption of crude oil for 1971–1975. Prices rose substantially between 1973 and 1974 due to an embargo. Suppose that world demand for oil follows the isoelastic heterogeneous demand model. Give the identified set for ε under each of the following further assumptions: (i) $\overline{Q}_{1973} = \overline{Q}_{1974}$, (ii) $\frac{\overline{Q}_{1973}}{\overline{Q}_{1972}} = \frac{\overline{Q}_{1974}}{\overline{Q}_{1973}}$, (iii) $\ln\left(\frac{\overline{Q}_{1974}}{\overline{Q}_{1973}}\right) \in [0, 0.1]$.

Table 3.1
Global price and quantity of crude oil, 1971–1975

Year t	Price P_t \$/barrel	Quantity consumed Q_t 1,000 barrels/day
1971	14.30	47,903
1972	15.35	51,440
1973	19.17	55,664
1974	60.81	54,911
1975	55.47	54,448

Source: bp (2021).
Notes: Prices are in 2020 USD.

Definition 3.5. The *(isoelastic) heterogeneous static monopoly model* holds that, in each market $t \in \{1, \ldots, T\}$,

$$P_t^* \in \arg\max_{P \in \mathbb{R}_{\geq 0}} \pi_t(P_t)$$

$$\pi_t(P) = Q_t(P_t)(P_t - C_t)$$

$$Q_t^* = Q_t(P_t^*)$$

for $C_t > 0$ and $Q_t(\cdot)$ satisfying the (isoelastic) heterogeneous demand model.

Exercise 3.7. Under the assumptions in exercise 3.6, if the isoelastic static monopoly model holds in 1974, what is the identified set for the monopolist's cost C_{1974}?

Exercise 3.8. Repeat exercise 3.6(iii) but with the assumption that $\ln\left(\frac{\overline{Q}_{1972}}{\overline{Q}_{1971}}\right) \in [0, 0.1]$. Contrast your answer with your answer to exercise 3.6(iii).

Exercise 3.9. Table 3.2 gives data on the world price and consumption of crude oil for 1980 and 1986. Consumption held fairly steady over this period. What about the demand function itself? To be more specific, under the assumptions in exercise 3.6(ii), what is the value of

$$\Delta = \ln Q_{1986}(P_{1980}) - \ln Q_{1980}(P_{1980})?$$

Can you offer an explanation for the direction of change in the demand function, i.e., the sign of Δ?

Table 3.2
Global price and quantity of crude oil, 1980 and 1986

Year t	Price P_t \$/barrel	Quantity consumed Q_t 1,000 barrels/day
1980	115.68	61,453
1986	34.08	61,168

Source: bp (2021).
Notes: Prices are in 2020 USD.

Definition 3.6. The *(isoelastic) partially homogeneous static monopoly model* is a special case of the (isoelastic) heterogeneous static monopoly with $C_t = C > 0$ for all $t \in \{1, ..., T\}$.

Exercise 3.10. A researcher has data $\{P_t^*, Q_t^*\}_{t=1}^T \in \mathbb{R}_{>0}$ from the isoelastic partially homogeneous static monopoly model. The researcher estimates a linear regression of $\ln Q_t$ on $\ln P_t$. Interpret the coefficient from this regression in terms of the model's primitives.

Exercise 3.11. Repeat exercise 3.10 but under the assumption that the data come from the isoelastic heterogeneous static monopoly model.

Note

1. That is, $\overline{\varepsilon} = Q_2'(\overline{P})$ for some $\overline{P} \in (P_1, P_2)$.

4

Production

An agent chooses a vector of inputs $\mathbf{X} \in \mathbb{R}^k_{\geq 0}$ with associated costs $\mathbf{W} \in \mathbb{R}^k_{\geq 0}$. From these inputs the agent produces a scalar quantity $Q = Q(\mathbf{X})$ of output determined by a production function $Q : \mathbb{R}^k_{\geq 0} \to \mathbb{R}_{\geq 0}$ that is differentiable and nondecreasing in all of its arguments. Output is transformed into value via a function $V : \mathbb{R}_{\geq 0} \to \mathbb{R}_{\geq 0}$ that is differentiable and strictly increasing. The agent takes costs $\mathbf{W}$ and the functions $Q(\cdot), V(\cdot)$ as given and maximizes the value of output produced, less the cost of inputs. For example, the agent might be an oil refinery that chooses a mix of materials, energy, labor, and other inputs to produce a refined product that is sold to market. Or the agent might be a manager of an ad campaign that chooses a mix of television ads, social media ads, and other inputs to influence sales of a good.

Definition 4.1. The *single-agent production model* holds that

$$\mathbf{X}^* \in \underset{\mathbf{X} \in \mathbb{R}^k_{\geq 0}}{\arg\max}\, V(Q(\mathbf{X})) - \mathbf{W}'\mathbf{X} \tag{4.1}$$

$$Q^* = Q(\mathbf{X}^*).$$

4.1 A Single Decision

Example 4.1. Nickerson et al. (2006) report the results of randomized field experiments undertaken by the Michigan Democratic Party to increase voter turnout. Nickerson et al. (2006, table 6) estimate that placing a door hanger on a potential voter's doorknob increases the probability the voter votes by 1.3 percentage points.

> **Question 4.1.** *Nickerson et al. (2006) also report the effect of reaching the voter with a phone call, and the effect of speaking to the voter face to face at their home. What are these effects?*
>
> *Pause to reflect. Write down your answer before continuing.*

Suppose that the Michigan Democratic Party acts according to the single-agent production model, with $\mathbf{X} \in \mathbb{R}^k_{\geq 0}$ the number of voters reached by each of k methods of contact, $\mathbf{W}$ the cost of each method, Q the number of voters turning out, and $V(\cdot)$ the value of these votes, given for example by a function of the probability of winning the election. The following observations are useful and follow immediately from the first-order necessary conditions of the problem in (4.1).

Fact 4.1. Any choice of inputs $\mathbf{X}^* \in \mathbb{R}^k_{\geq 0}$ arising from the single-agent production model must satisfy

$$V' Q_i\left(\mathbf{X}^*\right) = W_i$$

for all i such that $X_i^* > 0$. It follows that for any i,j such that $X_i^*, X_j^* > 0$, we have that

$$\frac{Q_i\left(\mathbf{X}^*\right)}{Q_j\left(\mathbf{X}^*\right)} = \frac{W_i}{W_j}.$$

Definition 4.2. Under the single-agent production model, the *equilibrium marginal return* to an input i such that $X_i^* > 0$ is $V' Q_i\left(\mathbf{X}^*\right)$.

Fact 4.2. Under the single-agent production model, for any i,j for which it is known that $X_i^*, X_j^* > 0$, the ratio of equilibrium marginal returns $Q_i\left(\mathbf{X}^*\right) / Q_j\left(\mathbf{X}^*\right)$ is identified from the ratio of costs W_i / W_j, and vice versa.

Fact 4.1 suggests a possible approach to answering question 4.1. Suppose there are $k = 3$ methods of contact, all used in equilibrium by the Michigan Democratic Party, so that $\mathbf{X}^* > 0$. Let method 1 be door hangers and let W_1 be its cost. If we can learn W_2 and W_3 then we can use fact 4.1 to answer question 4.1. Table 4.1 reports the number of voters reached per hour of a canvasser's time.

Table 4.1
Methods of contacting voters

Method	Voters reached per hour H_i	Effect on probability of vote Q_i (percentage points)
Door hanger	40	1.3
Phone call	18	?
Face-to-face	3	?

Source: Nickerson et al. (2006)

Answer question 4.1 in light of table 4.1.

Pause to reflect. Write down your answer before continuing.

Let W be the cost of one hour of a canvasser's time and let H_i be the number of voters reached per hour via method i. Then it may be reasonable to take $W_i = W/H_i$. Following this reasoning we have that, for any methods i, $Q_i(\mathbf{X}^*)/Q_1(\mathbf{X}^*) = W_i/W_1 = H_1/H_i$ and therefore that $Q_i(\mathbf{X}^*) = (H_1/H_i)\,Q_1(\mathbf{X}^*)$. From this expression we infer that the effect of a phone call on the probability of voting is $Q_2(\mathbf{X}^*) = (40/18)(1.3) \approx 2.9$ percentage points, and that the effect of a face-to-face contact on the probability of voting is $Q_3(\mathbf{X}^*) = (40/3)(1.3) \approx 17.3$ percentage points.

Question 4.2. *Can the information reported by Nickerson et al. (2006) be used to refute the single-agent production model?*

Pause to reflect. Write down your answer before continuing.

In the single-agent production model, if we observe both the relative returns to different inputs and their relative costs, we can use fact 4.1 to refute the model.

Fact 4.3. From data $\left\{Q_i(\mathbf{X}^*), W_i, \mathbf{1}_{X_i^*>0}\right\}_{i=1}^{k}$ it is possible to refute the single-agent production model, in particular if $Q_i(\mathbf{X}^*)/Q_j(\mathbf{X}^*) \neq W_i/W_j$ while $X_i^*, X_j^* > 0$.

Table 4.2 shows that the model is refuted in this case. However, the model appears to do a reasonable job approximating the returns, especially in light of the statistical and other uncertainty in the estimated returns and costs. Fact 4.2 and table 4.2 thus illustrate principle 2.

Table 4.2
Methods of contacting voters—returns

Method	Voters reached per hour H_i	Effect on probability of vote Q_i (percentage points)	
		Predicted	Estimated
Door hanger	40	1.3	1.3
Phone call	18	2.9	3.5
Face-to-face	3	17.3	18.1

Source: Nickerson et al. (2006)

Question 4.3. *Nickerson et al. (2006) write that "surprisingly, door hangers are just as cost-effective a means of increasing turnout as face-to-face contact."*

Are you surprised?

Question 4.4. *What is the value of a vote to the Michigan Democratic Party?*

Pause to reflect. Write down your answer before continuing.

Definition 4.3. Under the single-agent production model, the *equilibrium marginal value of output* is $V' = \frac{dV(Q)}{dQ}|_{Q=Q(\mathbf{X}^*)}$ and the *equilibrium marginal product* of an input i such that $X_i > 0$ is $Q_i(\mathbf{X}^*)$.

Fact 4.4. Under the single-agent production model, the equilibrium marginal value of output is identified from data $\{Q_i(\mathbf{X}^*), W_i\}$ for any i such that $X_i > 0$ is known to hold. In particular, $V' = W_i / Q_i(\mathbf{X}^*)$.

Intuitively, the ratio of an input's cost to its marginal product tells us the agent's willingness to pay for a unit of output. Applying fact 4.4 to the data in table 4.2 yields the estimated equilibrium marginal value of output in table 4.3.

Table 4.3
Estimated value of a vote

Method	Voters reached per hour H_i	Estimated effect on probability of vote Q_i (Percentage points)	Estimated value of a vote V' (Hours)	(Dollars)
Door hanger	40	1.3	1.92	28.85
Phone call	18	3.5	1.59	23.81
Face-to-face	3	18.1	1.84	27.62

Source: Nickerson et al. (2006)

Depending on the method of contact, obtaining one additional vote requires 1.59 to 1.92 hours of time. Nickerson et al. (2006) use a value of $W = 15$ for the cost of one hour, implying that the value of a marginal vote is between 23.81 and 28.85. If the model held exactly and the estimates were perfect, the estimated equilibrium marginal value would be identical across methods of contact. In practice, it is similar but not identical across the three methods.

Fact 4.4 and table 4.3 offer another illustration of principle 2. Economic ideas allow us to learn interesting parameters from a relatively small amount of information.

4.2 Many Decisions

In some cases we may observe a single agent making a similar decision in different time periods or markets.

Definition 4.4. The *repeated single-agent production model* holds that

$$\mathbf{X}_t^* \in \arg\max_{\mathbf{X}\in\mathbb{R}_{\geq 0}^k} V_t\left(Q_t\left(\mathbf{X}\right)\right) - \mathbf{W}_t'\mathbf{X} \tag{4.2}$$

$$Q_t^* = Q_t\left(\mathbf{X}^*\right)$$

for each period $t \in \{1, \ldots, T\}$.

An important special case of the repeated single-agent production model arises when output is sold to market at a constant price and the function $Q_t(\cdot)$ is identical across periods up to a multiplicative factor.

Definition 4.5. The *repeated single-agent multiplicative production model* is a special case of the repeated single-agent production model in which $V_t(Q) = Q$ for all $Q \in \mathbb{R}_{\geq 0}$ and $Q_t(\mathbf{X}) = A_t Q(\mathbf{X})$ for all $\mathbf{X} \in \mathbb{R}_{\geq 0}^k$, $t \in \{1, \ldots, T\}$, where $A_t \in \mathbb{R}_{\geq 0}$.

The repeated single-agent multiplicative production model and its variants have been widely studied in economics (e.g., Marschak and Andrews 1944) owing to their connection to the measurement of productivity A_t. We can learn some useful lessons by studying the special case of a single input, $k = 1$, and an isoelastic production function, $Q(X) = X^\alpha$.

Definition 4.6. The *repeated single-agent isoelastic production model* is a special case of the repeated single-agent multiplicative production model in which $k = 1$ and $Q(X) = X^\alpha$ for $\alpha \in (0, 1)$.

Under the repeated single-agent isoelastic production model, output takes a log-linear form:

$$\ln Q_t = \ln A_t + \alpha \ln X_t. \tag{4.3}$$

Question 4.5. *Under the repeated single-agent isoelastic production model, what is the coefficient from a regression of* $\ln Q_t$ *on* $\ln X_t$ *in data* $\{Q_t, X_t\}_{t=1}^T$*?*

Pause to reflect. Write down your answer before continuing.

Of course, whether the regression coefficient $\text{Coeff}(\ln Q_t, \ln X_t)$ exists depends on whether $\text{Var}(\ln X_t) > 0$. If it does exist, the coefficient is equal to

$$\text{Coeff}(\ln Q_t, \ln X_t) = \frac{\text{Cov}(\ln Q_t, \ln X_t)}{\text{Var}(\ln X_t)}.$$

Substituting equation 4.3, we find that

$$\text{Coeff}(\ln Q_t, \ln X_t) = \alpha + \text{Coeff}(\ln A_t, \ln X_t). \tag{4.4}$$

We recognize in equation 4.4 a version of the usual omitted variables bias formula.

Question 4.6. *Under the repeated single-agent isoelastic production model, is the parameter α identified from data* $\text{Coeff}(\ln Q_t, \ln X_t)$*?*

Pause to reflect. Write down your answer before continuing.

The answer is no. In fact, the parameter α is not identified even from the richer data $\{Q_t, X_t\}_{t=1}^T$.

Fact 4.5. Under the repeated single-agent isoelastic production model, the parameter α is not identified from data $\{Q_t, X_t\}_{t=1}^T$, and the model is not refuted from any data $\{Q_t, X_t\}_{t=1}^T$ with $Q_t, X_t > 0$ for all $t \in \{1, \dots, T\}$.

Exercise 4.8 proves fact 4.5 (below).

Perhaps equation 4.4 provides a route to identification of α, if only we could be sure that Coeff $(\ln A_t, \ln X_t) = 0$. Such a restriction is familiar as a common identifying assumption for linear regression models.

Assumption 4.1. We have that Coeff $(\ln A_t, \ln X_t) = 0$.

When considering a new economic assumption, it is a good idea to ask if the assumption is reasonable.

> **Question 4.7.** *Under the repeated single-agent isoelastic production model, is assumption 4.1 reasonable?*
>
> *Pause to reflect. Write down your answer before continuing.*

Under the single-agent isoelastic production model, if A_t, $W_t > 0$, we have that

$$\alpha A_t X_t^{\alpha-1} = W_t, \tag{4.5}$$

and so

$$\ln X_t = \frac{1}{1-\alpha}\ln\alpha + \frac{1}{1-\alpha}\ln A_t - \frac{1}{1-\alpha}\ln W_t. \tag{4.6}$$

The fact that $\ln X_t$ depends on $\ln A_t$ is a clue that assumption 4.1 may be awkward. Indeed, from equation 4.6, if assumption 4.1 holds, then it must be that $\text{Coeff}\,(\ln W_t, \ln A_t) = 1$. Though this situation is possible, it appears to be a strange coincidence.

Fact 4.6. Under the repeated single-agent isoelastic production model, assumption 4.1 implies that $\text{Coeff}\,(\ln W_t, \ln A_t) = 1$ when this coefficient exists.

Fact 4.6 illustrates an important principle.

Principle 7. *Restrictions on economic variables should be considered in the context of an economic model that governs those variables.*

Equation (4.6) and fact 4.6 suggest another route to learning about α.

Question 4.8. *Under the repeated single-agent isoelastic production model, what is the coefficient from a regression of* $\ln X_t$ *on* $\ln W_t$ *in data* $\{X_t, W_t\}_{t=1}^{T}$?

Pause to reflect. Write down your answer before continuing.

From equation 4.6 we have that

$$\text{Coeff}(\ln X_t, \ln W_t) = -\frac{1}{1-\alpha} + \frac{1}{1-\alpha}\,\text{Coeff}(\ln A_t, \ln W_t)\,. \tag{4.7}$$

If the forces affecting the cost W_t of the input and the productivity A_t of the agent are not directly related, then we may be prepared to suppose that Coeff $(\ln A_t, \ln W_t)$ is small in magnitude. Evidently, if Coeff $(\ln A_t, \ln W_t) \approx 0$, then Coeff $(\ln X_t, \ln W_t) \approx -\frac{1}{1-\alpha}$. Exercise 4.9 formalizes this intuition.

So far we have explored learning about α from either the variables Q_t and X_t or the variables X_t and W_t. What if we use data on all of these variables?

Question 4.9. *Under the repeated single-agent isoelastic production model, is the parameter α identified from data $\{Q_t, X_t, W_t\}_{t=1}^{T}$?*

Pause to reflect. Write down your answer before continuing.

Pick some period $t \in \{1, \ldots, T\}$ and suppose that $Q_t, X_t, W_t > 0$. From equation 4.5 we have that

$$\alpha = \frac{W_t X_t}{Q_t}.$$

It is therefore possible to learn α from a single period of data. It follows that the model is refuted if the value of α implied by two periods of data is different.

Fact 4.7. Under the repeated single-agent isoelastic production model, the parameter α is identified from data $\{Q_t, X_t, W_t\}_{t=1}^{T}$ if there is a single period with $Q_t, X_t, W_t > 0$. The model is refuted if there are two periods t, t' with $Q_t, X_t, W_t > 0$, $Q_{t'}, X_{t'}, W_{t'} > 0$ such that

$$\frac{W_t X_t}{Q_t} \neq \frac{W_{t'} X_{t'}}{Q_{t'}}.$$

Fact 4.7 illustrates both principle 2 and principle 6.

Exercises

Definition 4.7. The *single-agent allocation model* holds that

$$\mathbf{X}^* \in \underset{\left\{\mathbf{X} \in \mathbb{R}^k_{\geq 0} : \mathbf{W}'\mathbf{X} \leq M\right\}}{\arg\max} V\left(Q\left(\mathbf{X}\right)\right) \tag{4.8}$$

$$Q^* = Q\left(\mathbf{X}^*\right).$$

Exercise 4.1. Suppose that, rather than following the single-agent production model, the Michigan Democratic Party follows the single-agent allocation model, with M denoting the party's budget for voter mobilization efforts. Revisit questions 4.1, 4.2, and 4.4 under the single-agent allocation model.

Definition 4.8. The *single-agent eat-the-pie model* is a special case of the single-agent allocation model, with $V(Q) = Q$ for all $Q \in \mathbb{R}_{\geq 0}$ and $Q(\mathbf{X}) = \sum_{i=1}^{k} \delta^{i-1} q(X_i)$ for $\delta \in [0, 1]$ a discount factor and $q : \mathbb{R}_{\geq 0} \to \mathbb{R}_{\geq 0}$ a strictly increasing and differentiable felicity function. We may think of X_i as an agent's consumption in period i and W_i as the price of consumption in that period.

Exercise 4.2. Under the single-agent eat-the-pie model, is the discount factor δ identified from the data $\mathbf{X}^*, \mathbf{W}$? Justify your answer.

Definition 4.9. The *isoelastic single-agent eat-the-pie model* is a special case of the single-agent eat-the-pie model with $q(X) = \frac{X^{1-\rho}}{1-\rho}$ and parameters $(\delta, \rho) > 0$.

Exercise 4.3. Under the isoelastic single-agent eat-the-pie model, is the discount factor δ identified from the data $\mathbf{X}^*, \mathbf{W}$? Justify your answer.

Exercise 4.4. Under the isoelastic single-agent eat-the-pie model, describe sufficient conditions on W and k under which the parameters (δ, ρ) can be recovered from the coefficients of a linear regression based on the data $\mathbf{X}^*, \mathbf{W}$.

Exercise 4.5. Under the isoelastic single-agent eat-the-pie model, what is the R^2 of the regression you characterized in exercise 4.4?

Exercise 4.6. Shapiro (2005) studies the behavior of households who receive food stamps at the beginning of a benefit month and must allocate food consumption across the month. Shapiro (2005) reports that an ordinary least squares regression of the log of the cash value of food consumed on a given day on a variable counting the number of days into the benefit month has a coefficient of -0.0073. Interpret this coefficient in terms of the isoelastic single-agent eat-the-pie model.

Exercise 4.7. This exercise is based on Card and Krueger (1992). Time is continuous. An individual is in school from period 0 through period X and earns nothing while in school. After leaving school the individual earns $Q(X;S)$ per period forever, where $Q(\cdot;S)$ is a function that is increasing and differentiable in X and that may depend on the resources S of the individual's school district. For each of a set of districts d, an econometrician measures the resources S_d and the equilibrium marginal rate of return to schooling $R_d^* = Q'\left(X_d^*; S_d\right)/Q\left(X_d^*; S_d\right)$. The econometrician attempts to learn the productivity of school resources from the relationship between R_d^* and S_d. Analyze this approach. Justify it or critique it (or both).

Exercise 4.8. Prove fact 4.5.

Exercise 4.9. Under the repeated single-agent isoelastic production model, suppose that $|\text{Coeff}(\ln A_t, \ln W_t)| \leq B$ for some known $B \geq 0$ such that both $\text{Coeff}(\ln A_t, \ln W_t) = B$ and $\text{Coeff}(\ln A_t, \ln W_t) = -B$ are consistent with the data and model. Characterize the identified set for α given the data $\text{Coeff}(\ln X_t, \ln W_t)$.

Exercise 4.10. In the setting of exercise 4.9, if $B = 0$, what is the ratio $\frac{\text{Coeff}(\ln Q_t, \ln W_t)}{\text{Coeff}(\ln X_t, \ln W_t)}$ when these coefficients both exist?

Exercise 4.11. Bloom et al. (2012, table 2) estimate a model in which a firm's output is log-linear in its amount of information technology. Bloom et al. (2012) report that US-owned multinationals have an output elasticity with respect to the amount of information technology that is about 1.7 percentage points larger than the corresponding output elasticity for non-US-owned multinationals. In light of the repeated single-agent isoelastic production model, can you say anything about the relative intensity with which US-owned and non-US-owned multinationals should be expected to employ information technology?

Definition 4.10. The *static monopoly production model* holds that

$$\mathbf{X}^* \in \underset{\left\{\mathbf{X}\in\mathbb{R}^k_{\geq 0}\right\}}{\arg\max}\, P\left(Q\left(\mathbf{X}\right)\right) Q\left(\mathbf{X}\right) - \mathbf{W}'\mathbf{X} \tag{4.9}$$
$$Q^* = Q\left(\mathbf{X}^*\right)$$
$$P^* = P\left(Q^*\right).$$

where $P : \mathbb{R}_{\geq 0} \to \mathbb{R}_{\geq 0}$ is a strictly decreasing and differentiable inverse demand function and other definitions follow the single-agent production model.

Exercise 4.12. Under the static monopoly production model, the gain in surplus λ from an incremental (infinitesimal) increase in the quantity (see chapter 1) is identified from data $\{P^*, Q_i\left(\mathbf{X}^*\right), W_i\}$ consisting of the marginal product $Q_i\left(\mathbf{X}^*\right) > 0$ and marginal cost $W_i > 0$ of some input $i \in \{1, \ldots, k\}$ such that $X_i^* > 0$. Prove this.

5

Information

There are k states of the world, denoted $\mathcal{K} = \{1, \ldots, k\}$, each equally likely ex ante. An agent learns which cell p of a partition $\mathcal{P}(\mathcal{K})$ the realized state belongs to. The agent then chooses whether or not to take an action. If the agent does not take the action, denoted $a = 0$, the agent receives a payoff of 0. If the agent does take the action, denoted $a = 1$, the agent receives a payoff X_i that depends on the realized state i. The agent's payoff is then aX_i. We let $\mathbf{X} \in \mathbb{R}^k$ denote the vector of state-specific payoffs and assume that the agent knows $\mathbf{X}$. The agent maximizes their expected payoff and breaks ties in favor of taking the action.

For example, the agent might be a firm deciding whether or not to enter a market, as in chapter 2, but unlike in chapter 2, the market is of unknown size. If the market is too small, the variable profit from entry will not cover the entry cost, and the net profit will be negative. If the market is large enough, entry is profitable. The firm conducts market research and makes an imperfect assessment of the profitability of entry. For another example, the agent might be a municipal government deciding whether or not to undertake an infrastructure investment such as a bridge, after learning from feasibility studies. For another example, the agent might be a household deciding whether or not to purchase a risky asset such as a stock, after learning from a prospectus. And so on.

Question 5.1. *What is the agent's decision rule?*

Pause to reflect. Write down your answer before continuing.

A decision rule is a mapping from information to actions. Here the agent's information is the cell $p \in \mathcal{P}(\mathcal{K})$ of the partition $\mathcal{P}(\mathcal{K})$ in which the state is contained. A decision rule thus maps from the partition $\mathcal{P}(\mathcal{K})$ to the action space $\{0, 1\}$. An optimal decision rule takes the risky action, $a = 1$, whenever the expected payoff from doing so is weakly positive. To ease notation, let $\overline{X}_{\mathcal{S}} = \frac{1}{|\mathcal{S}|} \sum_{i \in \mathcal{S}} X_i$ denote the average payoff on any nonempty subset $\mathcal{S} \subseteq \mathcal{K}$ of the states.

Definition 5.1. The *risky decision model* holds that for each cell $p \in \mathcal{P}(\mathcal{K})$ of a partition $\mathcal{P}(\mathcal{K})$ of the states $\mathcal{K} = \{1, \ldots, k\}$, the agent chooses $a = 1$ if $\overline{X}_p \geq 0$, and $a = 0$ otherwise.

Figure 5.1 illustrates a state space and three possible partitions.

The risky decision model is flexible in some respects. For example, although the model assumes that each state is equally likely, this does not imply that each payoff X is equally likely, because we may have that $X_i = X_j$ for two states $i \neq j$. So, if 99% of the time the action has a payoff of 1, and 1% of the time it has a payoff of -10, we can represent this as a situation with $k = 100$ states, with $X_i = 1$ for $i \in \{1, \ldots, 99\}$ and $X_{100} = -10$.

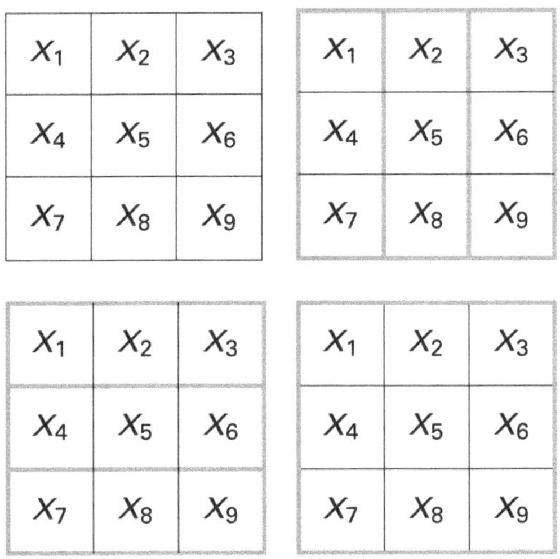

Figure 5.1
An example state space and partitions

Notes: The figure shows an example state space with $k = 9$ states, and three possible partitions $\mathcal{P}(\mathcal{K})$ of the state space $\mathcal{K} = \{1, \ldots, k\}$.

For another example, the model does not impose any structure on the payoffs. It is worthwhile to consider how far that flexibility goes.

Question 5.2. *Can the risky decision model accommodate a risk-averse agent?*

Pause to reflect. Write down your answer before continuing, and see exercise 5.1 for more.

5.1 Data on Actions and Payoffs

Suppose that the data consist of the agent's choice a_i in each state i, collected in the vector $\mathbf{a} \in \{0, 1\}^k$, as well as the state-specific payoffs $\mathbf{X} \in \mathbb{R}^k$. Such data may come from repeated observation of the same agent or from observation of different agents facing different realized states but with the same information structure (i.e., the same partition) and the same payoff structure.

Definition 5.2. The *perfect-information risky decision model* is an instance of the risky decision model in which $\mathcal{P}(\mathcal{K}) = \{\{1\}, \{2\}, \ldots, \{k\}\}$, i.e., the agent knows the realized state.

Question 5.3. *Can the data* $(\mathbf{a}, \mathbf{X})$ *ever refute the perfect-information risky decision model?*

Pause to reflect. Write down your answer before continuing.

Under the perfect-information risky decision model, the agent chooses $a = 1$ if and only if $X_i \geq 0$. Any violation of this condition refutes the model.

Fact 5.1. The data $(\mathbf{a}, \mathbf{X})$ refute the perfect-information risky decision model if and only if $a_i = 1$ for some $i \in \{1, \ldots, k\}$ for which $X_i < 0$.

It appears, then, that data on actions and payoffs can help us learn about the agent's information. Let us probe how far this approach can take us.

Question 5.4. *Is the partition $\mathcal{P}(\mathcal{K})$ identified from the data* $(\mathbf{a}, \mathbf{X})$*?*

Pause to reflect. Write down your answer before continuing.

Imagine data $(\mathbf{a},\mathbf{X})$ that are consistent with the perfect-information risky decision model. If $k \geq 3$, then there are at least two states i,j such that $a_i = a_j$. Under perfect information, the agent can tell these two states apart, i.e., $\{i\},\{j\} \in \mathcal{P}(\mathcal{K})$. But suppose the agent could not tell these two states apart, i.e., $\{i,j\} \in \mathcal{P}(\mathcal{K})$. The data $(\mathbf{a},\mathbf{X})$ are consistent with this alternative information structure because, by assumption, X_i, X_j are either both strictly negative or both weakly positive, and either way the agent's optimal action at states i and j does not depend on whether the agent can tell these two states apart.

This reasoning proves that the partition $\mathcal{P}(\mathcal{K})$ is not identified from the data $(\mathbf{a},\mathbf{X})$, because data consistent with perfect information will typically be consistent with imperfect information. We can take this argument further. Suppose that there is a partition $\mathcal{P}(\mathcal{K})$ with $|\mathcal{P}(\mathcal{K})| \geq 3$ that is consistent with some data $(\mathbf{a},\mathbf{X})$. Then there must be distinct cells p,q such that $a_i = a_j$ for all $i,j \in p \cup q$. It follows that either $\overline{X}_p, \overline{X}_q < 0$, in which case $\overline{X}_{p\cup q} < 0$, or $\overline{X}_p, \overline{X}_q \geq 0$, in which case $\overline{X}_{p\cup q} \geq 0$. Either way, if we construct a partition $\mathcal{P}'(\mathcal{K})$ that is identical to $\mathcal{P}(\mathcal{K})$ except that $(p \cup q) \in \mathcal{P}'(\mathcal{K})$, then partition $\mathcal{P}'(\mathcal{K})$ is also consistent with the data $(\mathbf{a},\mathbf{X})$. Since we can apply this logic repeatedly, and the set of states is finite, we have proved the following.

Fact 5.2. If the data $(\mathbf{a},\mathbf{X})$ do not refute the risky-decision model, then the data $(\mathbf{a},\mathbf{X})$ are consistent with a partition $\mathcal{P}(\mathcal{K})$ with $|\mathcal{P}(\mathcal{K})| = 2$ cells.

Fact 5.2 is intuitive: as there are only two possible actions, we cannot be sure that the agent can distinguish more than two groups of states. Exercise 5.2 continues this line of thinking.

5.2 Counterfactual Changes

When considering identification of model parameters, we should ask ourselves why we want to know.

> **Question 5.5.** *Suppose the data $(\mathbf{a},\mathbf{X})$ come from the risky decision model. What counterfactual changes might an economist be interested in?*
>
> *Pause to reflect. Write down your answer before continuing.*

By assumption, the data tell us how the agent acts in each possible state. So, predicting the agent's action under alternative states does not motivate an interest in identification of the information structure. Instead, an interest in identification of the information structure must come from an interest in predicting the effect of a counterfactual change in the environment.

One change whose effects we may be interested in is a change in the agent's information, for example due to providing the firm with superior market research. Can we identify the effect of such a change? Let us pose the question more concretely.

Question 5.6. *Suppose the data* $(\mathbf{a}, \mathbf{X})$ *come from the risky decision model. Can we identify the effect of providing the agent with perfect information, i.e., the actions* $\mathbf{a}'$ *that would arise, given the same payoffs, under the perfect information risky decision model?*

Pause to reflect. Write down your answer before continuing.

Of course we can. Under the perfect information risky decision model, $a_i^* = \mathbf{1}_{X_i \geq 0}$. It follows that $\mathbf{a}^*$ is a function of $\mathbf{X}$, and so is identified from the data $(\mathbf{a}, \mathbf{X})$. This is an example of a more general fact.

Fact 5.3. Let $\mathcal{P}(\mathcal{K})$ be the agent's partition and let $\mathcal{P}'(\mathcal{K})$ be some counterfactual partition of interest. Under the risky decision model, the change in the action profile, $\mathbf{a}' - \mathbf{a}$, that would result from switching from the factual partition to the counterfactual partition is identified from the data $(\mathbf{a}, \mathbf{X})$.

Fact 5.3 is a corollary of the statement proved in Exercise 5.3.

Another change whose effects we may be interested in is a change in the payoffs.

Question 5.7. *Suppose the data* $(\mathbf{a}, \mathbf{X})$ *come from the risky decision model. Can we identify the effect of changing the payoffs, i.e., the actions* $\mathbf{a}'$ *that would arise, given the same information structure, under alternative payoffs* $\mathbf{X}'$*?*

Pause to reflect. Write down your answer before continuing.

Recall our example of the data $(\mathbf{a}, \mathbf{X})$ that are consistent with the perfect information risky decision model. For any states i, j such that $a_i = a_j$, the data are consistent with a partition $\overline{\mathcal{P}}(\mathcal{K})$ reflecting perfect information, $\{i\}, \{j\} \in \overline{\mathcal{P}}(\mathcal{K})$, and with a partition $\underline{\mathcal{P}}(\mathcal{K})$ reflecting imperfect information, $\{i, j\} \in \underline{\mathcal{P}}(\mathcal{K})$.

These two partitions are equally consistent with the data $(\mathbf{a}, \mathbf{X})$ but have different implications for the actions $\mathbf{a}'$ arising under alternative payoffs $\mathbf{X}'$. Suppose, for example, that $X_i, X_j < 0$ so that $a_i = a_j = 0$. Consider alternative payoffs $\mathbf{X}'$ that coincide with $\mathbf{X}$ except that $X_j' \in \left[0, \frac{X_i}{2}\right)$. The agent's action under the alternative payoffs $\mathbf{X}'$ depends on the partition. If the partition is $\overline{\mathcal{P}}(\mathcal{K})$, then $a_j' = 1$. If the partition is $\underline{\mathcal{P}}(\mathcal{K})$, then $a_j' = 0$. This counterexample proves the following.

Fact 5.4. Under the risky decision model, the change in the action profile $\mathbf{a}' - \mathbf{a}$ that would result from switching from the factual payoffs $\mathbf{X}$ to counterfactual payoffs $\mathbf{X}'$ is not identified from the data $(\mathbf{a}, \mathbf{X})$.

The counterexample also illustrates a useful economic intuition.

Intuition 5.1. A less informed agent tends to be less responsive to changes in realized payoffs.

Exercises 5.4, 5.13, and 5.14 explore intuition 5.1 further.

5.3 Strategic Behavior

In many economic situations the payoff received by one agent depends on the actions of another. For example, the payoff to a firm from entering a market may depend on which other firms also enter it. Here we extend the risky decision model to accommodate these situations.

There are again k states of the world, denoted $\mathcal{K} = \{1, \ldots, k\}$, each equally likely ex ante. Each agent $n \in \{1, \ldots, N\}$ learns which cell p of a partition $\mathcal{P}_n(\mathcal{K})$ the realized state belongs to. The agent then chooses whether or not to take an action. If the agent does not take the action, denoted $a = 0$, the agent receives a payoff of 0. If the agent does take the action, denoted $a = 1$, the agent receives a payoff $X_{i,n}(\mathbf{a}_{i,-n})$ that depends on the realized state i and the actions $\mathbf{a}_{i,-n}$ of the other agents. The agent's payoff is then $aX_{i,n}(\mathbf{a}_{i,-n})$. We let $\mathbf{X}_n$: $\left(\{0, 1\}^k\right)^{n-1} \to \mathbb{R}^k$ denote agent n's payoff function and assume that the partitions $\mathcal{P}_1(\mathcal{K}), \ldots, \mathcal{P}_N(\mathcal{K})$ are commonly known. Each agent maximizes their expected payoff, taking the actions of other agents as given, and breaking ties in favor of taking the action.

To ease notation, let $\overline{X}_{\mathcal{S},n}(\mathbf{a}_{-n}) = \frac{1}{|\mathcal{S}|} \sum_{i \in \mathcal{S}} X_{i,n}(\mathbf{a}_{i,-n})$ denote the average payoff of agent n, given the action profile $\mathbf{a}_{-n}$ of the other agents, on any nonempty subset $\mathcal{S} \subseteq \mathcal{K}$ of the states.

Definition 5.3. The *risky game model* holds that for each agent $n \in \{1, \ldots, N\}$ and each cell $p \in \mathcal{P}_n(\mathcal{K})$ of a partition $\mathcal{P}_n(\mathcal{K})$ of the states $\mathcal{K} = \{1, \ldots, k\}$, the agent chooses $a = 1$ if $\overline{X}_{p,n}(\mathbf{a}_{-n}) \geq 0$, and $a = 0$ otherwise.

Implicit in this definition is that each agent knows each other agent's action profile, but not necessarily each other agent's action.

Incorporating multiple agents allows us to consider comparisons among them.

Question 5.8. *Suppose the data* $\{(\mathbf{a}_n, \mathbf{X}_n)\}_{n=1}^{N}$ *come from the risky game model. Could we ever refute that some agent n is more informed than some other agent* n'*?*

Pause to reflect. Write down your answer before continuing.

First we should say what it means for one agent to be more informed than another.

Definition 5.4. Agent n is more informed than agent n' if and only if $\mathcal{P}_n(\mathcal{K})$ is finer than $\mathcal{P}_{n'}(\mathcal{K})$. Agent n is strictly more informed than agent n' if and only if agent n is more informed than agent n' and agent n' is not more informed than agent n.

Recall that in any state i, agents n and n' each learn which cell $p_n \in \mathcal{P}_n(\mathcal{K}), p_{n'} \in \mathcal{P}_{n'}(\mathcal{K})$ the state belongs to. Under definition 5.4, if agent n is more informed than agent n', then $i \in p_n \subseteq p_{n'}$. Intuitively, this means that agent n knows what cell agent n' learns, and hence, agent n knows what agent n' knows.

With this definition in hand, it is easy to see that some data can refute that agent n is more informed than agent n'. Suppose, for example, that $X_{i,n}(\mathbf{a}_{i,-n}) = X_i$ for all i and n, so that each agent faces a common payoff that does not depend on the other agents' actions. Then if, for some agent n', we have that $a_{in'} = \mathbf{1}_{X_i \geq 0}$ for all $i \in \{1, \ldots, k\}$, we can refute that agent n is more informed than agent n' if $\mathbf{a}_n \neq \mathbf{a}_{n'}$. Exercise 5.16 proves this. Intuitively, when different agents face the same choice problem, a more informed agent takes actions that deliver higher ex post payoffs. Exercise 5.17 considers the strategic implications when one agent is more informed than another.

Exercises

Example 5.1. A household has wealth $W > 0$, of which it can choose to invest an amount $F \in (0, W)$ either in a riskless asset, or a risky asset. If the household invests in the riskless asset, it receives a gross return of $R_0 \geq 1$ regardless of the state, for a gross payment of $R_0 F$. If the household invests in the risky asset, the household receives a gross return of $R_i \geq 0$ in state i, for a gross payment of $R_i F$. The household has a strictly increasing and concave utility function $U(\cdot)$ over its final wealth, and maximizes its expected utility, breaking ties in favor of investing in the risky asset.

Exercise 5.1. State whether the payoffs in example 5.1 are a special case of those in the risky decision model, and provide a proof.

Exercise 5.2. The data $(\mathbf{a}, \mathbf{X}) \in \{0, 1\}^k \times \mathbb{R}^k, \mathbf{a} \neq \mathbf{1}$, are consistent with the single-agent risky decision model if and only if $\mathbf{a} \cdot \mathbf{X} \geq 0$ and $(1 - \mathbf{a}) \cdot \mathbf{X} < 0$. Prove this.

Exercise 5.3. Under the risky decision model, from data $(\mathbf{a}, \mathbf{X})$ we can identify the optimal action profile $\mathbf{a}'$ under any known partition $\mathcal{P}'(\mathcal{K})$. Prove this.

Exercise 5.4. Consider an instance of the risky decision model with payoffs $\mathbf{X}$ and partition $\mathcal{P}(\mathcal{K})$, and suppose that for a given state i we have $a_i = 0$. Consider the alternative payoffs $\mathbf{X}(\Delta) = \mathbf{X} + \Delta \mathbf{e}_i$ for Δ a scalar and $\mathbf{e}_i$ the ith standard basis vector, so that $\mathbf{X}(\Delta)$ increments the payoff in state i by an amount Δ. Characterize the smallest value $\underline{\Delta}$ of Δ so that, in the risky decision model with payoffs $\mathbf{X}(\Delta)$ and partition $\mathcal{P}(\mathcal{K})$, we have that $a_i = 1$. Relate your answer to intuition 5.1.

Definition 5.5. The *deductible choice model* is an instance of the risky decision model in which a household has initial wealth W and chooses whether to adopt a high-deductible plan, $a = 1$, or a low-deductible plan, $a = 0$. The deductible is $D(a) = \underline{D}(1-a) + a\overline{D}$, where $\underline{D} < \overline{D}$ describe the low and high deductibles, respectively. The states $\mathcal{K}$ are partitioned into a nonempty set of loss states $\mathcal{L} \subseteq \mathcal{K}$ and a nonempty set of non–loss states $\mathcal{K} \setminus \mathcal{L}$. In a loss state, the household faces a loss of $L > \overline{D}$, of which any amount over $D(a)$ is paid by the insurer, and the rest is paid by the household. In all states, the household pays a premium $P(a) = \underline{P}(1-a) + a\overline{P}$, where $\underline{P} > \overline{P}$ describe the premiums for the low and high-deductible plans, respectively. The household has a utility function $U(\cdot)$ that is strictly increasing in final wealth.

Exercise 5.5. Cast the deductible choice model into the notation of the risky decision model by characterizing the payoffs X_i.

Exercise 5.6. Based on your answer to exercise 5.5, under what conditions is the low-deductible plan undominated, in the sense that there exists *some* state under which $X_i < 0$?

Exercise 5.7. The data in table 5.1 are from a study of deductible choice in automobile insurance. Is the low-deductible plan undominated according to the condition you derived in exercise 5.6?

Exercise 5.8. The data on plan choice in table 5.1 come from a sample of households. What share of households choose the high-deductible plan in a loss state? In a non–loss state?

Table 5.1
Deductible choices and claims in a sample of automobile insurance policies

Deductible choice	Share of plans	Deductible	Premium	Loss frequency
Low	0.178	875	3,381	0.309
High	0.822	1,453	3,189	0.232

Source: Cohen and Einav (2007, table 2A)

Exercise 5.9. Imagine that each household may have a different utility function $U(\cdot)$. Are the data in table 5.1 consistent with the deductible choice model under perfect information? Prove your answer.

Exercise 5.10. Imagine that each household may have a different utility function $U(\cdot)$ but all face the same state space, i.e., the same number of loss and non–loss states. Are the data in table 5.1 consistent with the deductible choice model under *no* information, i.e., where each household's partition $\mathcal{P}(\mathcal{K})$ consists of a single cell $\mathcal{K}$? Prove your answer.

Exercise 5.11. Imagine that all households have the same utility function $U(\cdot)$ and all face the same state space. Are the data in table 5.1 consistent with the deductible choice model if all households face the same information structure, i.e., the same partition $\mathcal{P}(\mathcal{K})$ of the state space? Prove your answer.

Exercise 5.12. Repeat Exercise 5.11 under the assumption that the function $U(\cdot)$ is strictly increasing and linear.

Exercise 5.13. Mas and Pallais (2017, figure 1) found that, when given a binary choice between a less flexible job that pays a standard wage, and a more flexible one that pays \$5 less, 30 percent of applicants chose the more flexible job. The authors argue that this value may overstate the preference for flexibility, because a share $\alpha \in [0, 1]$ of applicants were simply not paying attention to the details of the jobs. Can you formalize the authors' argument under the risky decision model? Is there a value of α such that the data do not refute that all applicants strictly prefer the less flexible job?

Exercise 5.14. Mas and Pallais (2017, figure 1) also gave applicants a binary choice between a less flexible job that pays a standard wage, and a more flexible one that pays \$5 *more*. Suppose that, in this case, all applicants strictly prefer the more flexible job. Under the conditions you derived in exercise 5.13, what percent of applicants would you predict to have chosen the more flexible job? Relate your answer to intuition 5.1.

Table 5.2
Motel formats in a population of highway exits

Configuration	Probability
Both low quality	0.27
One low quality, one high quality	0.42
Both high quality	0.31

Source: Mazzeo (2002, table 4)

Definition 5.6. The *product type model* is a special case of the risky game model in which there are two agents, $N = 2$, with identical partitions, $\mathcal{P}_1(\mathcal{K}) = \mathcal{P}_2(\mathcal{K}) = \mathcal{P}(\mathcal{K})$, and agent n's payoff from taking action $a = 1$ in state i is given by $X_i = X_i^0$ if $a_{i,-n} = 0$ and $X_i = X_i^1$, if $a_{i,-n} = 1$, where $X_i^1 - X_i^0 = d \in \mathbb{R}$.

Exercise 5.15. The data in table 5.2 are from a study of motel markets along highway exits in the US. Here, the agents $n \in \{1, 2\}$ are motel operators and the action $a_i = 1$ denotes adopting a high-quality format. Under the product type model, what is the identified set for the parameter d?

Exercise 5.16. Suppose that the data $\{(\mathbf{a}_n, \mathbf{X}_n)\}_{n=1}^{N}$ come from the risky game model, that $X_{i,n}(\mathbf{a}_{i,-n}) = X_i$ for all i, n, and $\mathbf{a}_{i,-n}$, and that for some agent n', we have that $a_{in'} = \mathbf{1}_{X_i \geq 0}$ for all $i \in \{1, \ldots, k\}$. If, for some agent n, we have that $\mathbf{a}_n \neq \mathbf{a}_{n'}$, then agent n is not more informed than agent n'. Prove this.

Definition 5.7. The *risky entry game* is a special case of the risky game model in which there are two firms, $N = 2$, each of which must decide whether to enter a given market ($a = 1$) or not ($a = 0$) at a known cost of F. The size of the market V_i depends on the state. If both firms enter, they split the market, each earning revenues of $V_i/2$. If one firm enters, it earns revenue of V_i. Thus, $X_i = V_i - F - (V_i/2)\, a_{-i}$.

Exercise 5.17. This exercise is based on Goldfarb and Xiao (2011). Consider a special case of the risky entry game in which $V_i \in \{V_L, V_H\}$ with $0 < V_L < F < V_H$ and $V_H + V_L < 2F$. One firm has partition $\underline{\mathcal{P}}(\mathcal{K})$ and one has partition $\overline{\mathcal{P}}(\mathcal{K})$, where these are given below. Suppose the data consist of the unique tuples $(V_i, a_{i,1}, a_{i,2})$. From these data, could you ever tell whether it is firm 1 or firm 2 that is more informed?

State i	Market size V_i	Cell of $\underline{\mathcal{P}}(\mathcal{K})$	Cell of $\overline{\mathcal{P}}(\mathcal{K})$
1	V_L	p_1	p_1
2	V_L	p_2	p_2
3	V_H	p_2	p_3
4	V_H	p_3	p_4

References

Becker, Gary S. 2007. *Economic Theory*. 2nd ed. New York: Routledge.

BIA Advisory Services. 2021. "Investing in Radio Market Report." https://www.bia.com/Images/Products/Radio%20Market%20Report%20Info.pdf

Bloom, Nicholas, Raffaella Sadun, and John Van Reenen. 2012. "Americans Do IT Better: US Multinationals and the Productivity Miracle." *American Economic Review* 102 (1): 167–201.

bp. 2021. "Statistical Review of World Energy." https://www.bp.com/content/dam/bp/business-sites/en/global/corporate/xlsx/energy-economics/statistical-review.

Card, David, and Alan B. Krueger. 1992. "Does School Quality Matter? Returns to Education and the Characteristics of Public Schools in the United States." *Journal of Political Economy* 100 (1): 1–40.

Cohen, Alma, and Liran Einav. 2007. "Estimating Risk Preferences from Deductible Choice." *American Economic Review* 97 (3): 745–788.

Connor, John M. 2008. "The Great Global Vitamins Conspiracies, 1985–1999." May, https://ssrn.com/abstract=885968.

EuroMillions. 2022. "EuroMillions Prizes and Prize Fund Distribution." https://www.euro-millions.com/prizes.

Goldfarb, Avi, and Mo Xiao. 2011. "Who Thinks about the Competition? Managerial Ability and Strategic Entry in US Local Telephone Markets." *American Economic Review* 101 (7): 3130–3161.

Igami, Mitsuru, and Takuo Sugaya. 2021. "Replication Package for: Measuring the Incentive to Collude: The Vitamin Cartels, 1990–1999." https://doi.org/10.5281/zenodo.5104830.

Igami, Mitsuru, and Takuo Sugaya. 2022. "Measuring the Incentive to Collude: The Vitamin Cartels, 1990–1999." *The Review of Economic Studies* 89 (3): 1460–1494.

Jaffe, Sonia, Robert Minton, Casey B. Mulligan, and Kevin M. Murphy. 2019. *Chicago Price Theory*. Princeton, NJ: Princeton University Press.

Marschak, Jacob. 1950. "Statistical Inference in Economics: An Introduction." In *Statistical Inference in Dynamic Economic Models*, edited by Tjalling C. Koopmans, Chap. 1. New York: John Wiley & Sons.

Marschak, Jacob, and William H. Andrews. "Random Simultaneous Equations and the Theory of Production." *Econometrica*. 12 (3-4): 143–205.

Mas, Alexandre, and Amanda Pallais. 2017. "Valuing Alternative Work Arrangements." *American Economic Review* 107 (12): 3722–3759.

Mazzeo, Michael J. 2002. "Product Choice and Oligopoly Market Structure." *RAND Journal of Economics* 43 (2): 221–242.

Nickerson, David W., Ryan D. Friedrichs, and David C. King. 2006. "Partisan Mobilization Campaigns in the Field: Results from a Statewide Turnout Experiment in Michigan." *Political Research Quarterly* 59 (1): 85–97.

RadioInsight. 2022. "Boston Nielsen Audio PPM Monthly Ratings." https://radioinsight.com/ratings/boston.

Sanders, Tony. 2001. "Spring 2001 Ratings Report." *Duncan's American Radio* 26 (1): 1–398.

Shapiro, Jesse M. 2005. "Is There a Daily Discount Rate? Evidence from the Food Stamp Nutrition Cycle." *Journal of Public Economics* 89 (2): 303–325.

Smith, James L. 2009. "World Oil: Market or Mayhem?" *Journal of Economic Perspectives* 23 (3): 145–164.

Steiner, Peter O. 1952. "Program Patterns and Preferences, and the Workability of Competition in Radio Broadcasting." *Quarterly Journal of Economics* 66 (2): 194–223.

Index

Page numbers followed by *f* denote a figure; a *t* denotes a table.

Publisher contact:
The MIT Press
Massachusetts Institute of Technology
77 Massachusetts Avenue, Cambridge, MA 02139
mitpress.mit.edu

EU Authorised Representative:
Easy Access System Europe, Mustamäe tee 50,
10621 Tallinn, Estonia
gpsr.requests@easproject.com

Printed by Integrated Books International,
United States of America